An
Attitude of Love

On Life And Relationships

Revised Second Edition

An
Attitude of Love

on Life and Relationships
Revised Second Edition

By

Samuel L. Brown, MSW

Accreistre Publishing Company

Florida

Accreistre Publishing Company
Post Office Box 1916
Dade City, Florida 33526-1916.

The names, characters, and events used to portray clients for cases analysis in this book are fictitious. Any similarity to real persons, living or dead, is coincidental and not intended by the author.

The goal of this book is life and relationship education. This is not medical or therapeutic advice. For help with personal counseling and health needs, please consult your qualified medical or mental health provider.

Library of Congress Cataloging-in-Publication Data

Brown, Samuel L.
An Attitude of Love: On life and relationships/by Samuel L. Brown—2nd ed. Revised.

Library of Congress Control Number: 2006902632

10 digit- ISBN: 0-9701839-3-3
13 digit- ISBN: 978-0-9701839-3- 4

Printed in the United States of America

Cover photo: Samuel and Deborah Brown
Photographer: Casares Photography

To

Deborah

my soul mate for 25 years.

For her unwavering support, patience,
and sharing the most rewarding
relationship of my life.

Acknowledgements

Most of the information in this book is based on practical experience as a social worker and my subjective knowledge and experiences as a son, brother, uncle, husband, father, and an ordinary human being. Much of my knowledge and some of the information shared in this book are also based on accumulated research findings in many different fields of psychology, human behavior, and social work. Therefore, directly or indirectly, I owe a debt of gratitude to numerous scientists, researchers, and scholars from many different academic fields. Some of them, if not all, are noted in the references and suggested readings.

I would also like to extend my appreciation and heart warming thanks to everyone who helped make the publication of my first book a success. To my wife Deborah, for all her supportive efforts and patience; my cousins Lester and Lillian Seays whose encouragement inspired me to become a published author as a contributing writer with Onyx magazine. To Clydeana Weatherspoon Willis for her assistance—proofreading, designing charts, and book promotions. To my sister Lois Prime for her knowledge, time, and book sales.

For encouragement and support, great or small, I am especially indebted to Jacqueline Davis, Renee Broome, Megan Steele, Thelma Coote-Hampton, Maria Dukes, Mildred Ramsey, Belinda Drake, Reginald, Cherry, and Genevia Peterson, Brad Vogel, and the East Hernando Branch Library staff (Amanda and Lucille).

Special thanks to all the ministers and members who invited me to their church to give a talk and book signing. I would also like to record my gratitude to Margie Samuel of the East End Baptist Church, Bridgeport, Connecticut; Rev. Eddie A. Nunn of Macedonia M.B. Church, Zephyrhills, Fl., and the members of the Brotherhood who attended the workshop I conducted on "Fatherhood." To the Christian Church of

Love in Webster, Fl.; Rev. Moses E. Freeman, Jr., of St. Mark M.B. Church, Plant City, Fl.; Rev. Willie L. Fowler, of New Palms River C.O.G.I., Tampa, Fl.; Bishop John Shingle and Rev. Dr. Samuel Shingle of Solid Rock Deliverance Church, Jacksonville, Fl.; and Rev. Joy Gallmon, of Allen Temple AME, Brooksville, Fl.

Thanks to all the churches and ministers who welcomed me with Christian love and support. I am indeed grateful and feel blessed by all of you.

Many thanks to everyone who purchased and read the first edition critically and dared to share their honest and constructive opinions, all of whom, help paved the way for the publication of this revised and expanded second edition.

Preface To The Second Edition

This second edition of Notes on Life and Relationships has been extensively revised and expanded as a response to the many ideas and questions that readers brought to the author since the publication of the first edition. Including the suggestion for a new title, hence, An Attitude of Love: On Life and Relationships.

After the publication of *Notes on Life and Relationships*, several people requested I write a follow-up, with specific requests to expand on the examples used. Many of the readers said they learned something about themselves and others from the varied examples cited.

In addition to the new title, this edition includes a glossary to help readers understand certain unavoidable terminology and a reference and suggested reading list. I have also tried to correct errors as well as expand on the various short-stories for further explanations of different human interactions.

When most people describe their idea of living a rewarding life, they talk about having, or their desire to have, peace of mind, a happy marriage, a healthy and supportive family, and close friends.

This book should be read by every individual experiencing behavioral conflicts in their interpersonal relationships, by everyone contemplating marriage, by married couples young and old, by parents or expecting parents, students, marriage and family counselors, and educators.

It was heart warming when readers purchased two or more of the first edition to give as a gift(s) to a loved one. I think readers will find this revised and expanded second edition to be much more of an enjoyable reading. And a book they would want to share with family members, friends, and coworkers.

Dade City, Florida   Samuel L. Brown, MSW
February 20, 2006

Preface To The First Edition

As a student of history and a professionally trained social worker, I have spent the majority of my life studying human relationships, activities, and interests. I agree with the widely held view that relationships form one of the most important aspects of life.

I have often pondered the important questions about life, searched for the true meaning of love, and questioned the difference between love and sex. This book is a product of my search for answers.

Much new research and writing about the study of human relationships are constantly being produced. The field of human behavior is gaining new prominence, however, the existing research and writing on the topics of life, marriage, parenting, love, and sex are quite voluminous, and accessible.

Throughout my social work career, I have heard many ask "What is the meaning of life?" Why do people behave the way they do?" "How can I make my marriage work? "What can I do to help other people understand me?" "Is there life after death?"

I have tried to write this book in a way that would help readers understand some of the basic principles of human relationships, and how different attitudes and behaviors are formed. I hope it will help the average layman to understand better why human beings act as they do, and realize that everything we do has a reason.

By sharing information about my social work background and using examples to illustrate various types of attitudes and behaviors. I have also tried to make this book a personal one that will involve readers in an active and meaningful way.

Dade City, Florida   Samuel Lee Brown, MSW
February 21, 2003

Table of Contents

Introduction

This revised and expanded second edition of *Notes On Life and Relationships*, under the new title, **An Attitude of Love** is a collection of essays and short-stories highlighting the importance of nurturing relationships. A list of references and suggested readings with a glossary has also been added.

Most of the essays derived from my notes recorded during preparation for lectures, seminars, and workshops conducted since 1969, when I began my career as a student social worker. The short stories are about various aspects of life and relationships.

The focus of this book is on family life—exploring some of the everyday questions, views, and concerns shared by others during many of my group discussions about life, love, marriage, sex, family, parenting, and fatherhood.

The goal of this book is to share information about human behavior in an unscientific, but informative and entertaining style of writing.

In addition to my personal search for answers, I have, in some small measure, attempted to answer many of my former clients' questions about personal and interpersonal relationships, not so much in terms of scientific facts, but more in terms of information relevant to their unique social experiences.

There were numerous questions about why people behave as they do, and about the way people form or maintain social relationships. Many wanted to know, how to determine if he or she is truly in love, what constitutes a healthy marriage, and how to overcome emotional or physical abuse to start living a rewarding life.

First, in order for anyone to understand others we must learn how to understand ourselves and recognize how our attitudes and behavior determines our destiny.

Although the questions regarding whether life begin at conception or at birth are important questions. This book focus only on events, conditions, and relationships of human beings during the time between birth and death.

Starting at birth, every human being is first identified by gender, family affiliation, or some type of label—male/female, son/daughter, brother/sister, nephew/niece, or cousin, thereby immediately assigning us to different roles in life. Such labels often distinguishes each person as an individual until he or she enters the holy bond of matrimony, called Marriage—the legal union of a man and a woman who subsequently are identified by their new role as a husband and wife. After the wedding, the husband and wife are expected to change their status by having children.

Following the birth of their first child, a husband and wife assume the role of parents and are identified as a father and mother respectively.

In many cases, these new fathers and mothers are concerned about developing effective parenting skills in an effort to raise their children to become healthy, responsible, and productive members of society.

As one of America's most important social institutions, the family has had responsibility for providing security and protection for children and shaping their personalities into productive citizens.

As a marriage and family counselor, I worked with various types of families, from different socio-economic, racial, and religious backgrounds. There appears to be a common thread linking all families together—the care and concern for the welfare of children.

The chapter on family is a collection of fictitious short stories. These stories were written in an effort to describe the varied dynamics of ethnic American families.

No one, questions the role of motherhood, and only

because of certain circumstances does anyone question the natural bond between a mother and her child, but what about the role of fathers. There are numerous responsible and caring men who feel anxious about fatherhood. Some of these fathers are finally being accepted for their nurturing contributions to their children, beyond recognition as a good provider, or "bread winner."

Chapter VI, is entitled, *The Joy of Fatherhood,* which includes a "tough love" talk about fatherhood and men's responsibilities towards their children.

The essay on *Attention Deficit-Disorder (ADD),* in chapter VIII, *Coping with life crises* was originally written for my June, 1990 presentation at Christ Disciple Church in Bridgeport, Connecticut. It was revised for my November 16, 1994 presentation before the Florida Chapter of the National Association of Social Workers (NASW), in Hudson, Florida.

On September 1, 2001, I delivered a presentation at Mt. Pleasant Missionary Baptist Church, in Trilby, Florida, on Attention-Deficit/Hyperactivity Disorder (AD/HD). My talk included information from my original lecture, in addition to recent research data, and treatment options.

The short article on ADD, in this book was revised to help parents and families better understand and recognize some of the symptoms of ADHD. I have also tried to convey the necessity for early evaluations and treatment of young people confronting various behavioral problems.

Frequently, when many people make reference to the term, *Relationship,* they think of sexual activities or sexual involvement between two people, or relations based solely on birth, marriage, or family ties.

If a relationship is a condition involving an emotional, psychological, verbal, or physical connection between two or more people. Then their emotional, spiritual, and financial involvement or interaction would appear to also constitute a relationship.

In recent years, the word *relationship* refers to the way people are connected to each other based on how they communicate or behave towards one another, regardless of whether they are related by blood ties or working on a temporary project together. This definition includes the existence of all human interactions as the basis for a relationship. Between parent and child, husband and wife, siblings, extended relatives, friends, and coworkers. Even the service component between a social worker and client, doctor and patient, teacher and student, also constitute a relationship.

For the contents of this book the phrase "quality of life" will refer to the connection of a strong positive bond between the words *life* and *relationships.* The strong positive bond between human beings, which contributes towards developing and maintaining harmony or balance between mind, body, and soul—mentally, physically, and psychologically.

Again, the goal of this book is to provide personal and shared views about life and relationship information. This is not medical or therapeutic advice. For help with personal counseling and health needs, please consult your qualified medical or mental health provider.

Excerpts from the chapters on marriage, parenting, fatherhood, attention deficit disorder, and depression have been previously published in the Onyx Magazine of Florida.

Chapter I

NOTES ON LIFE

How many times have you asked or heard someone else ask "What is life? Why are we here? Who created human beings? Why do people fall in love, marry, form families, and communities? Why are human beings monogamous? Why do people behave as they do? Is the life of every individual predetermined or do human beings really have control over their lives? What makes life worthwhile or rewarding? Are you enjoying your life, or are you just existing?

Discussions about life, often reminds me of a young woman struggling with depression while contemplating suicide. She asked, "What is life all about anyway?" and "Why was I born?"

In her passionate plea for help she said, "I didn't ask to be born."

She was born to a drug addicted mother, abandoned at the age of five, and lived in eight different foster care homes before her 12th birthday.

After living most of her life in-and-out of institutions and foster placements, she had, nevertheless, graduated from high school and was living independently with gainful employment.

Throughout her childhood and early adult life, she had experienced behavioral and emotional problems with a low tolerance for frustration. Her inability to manage stress effectively also made it difficult for her to establish or maintain a stable or secure relationship with others. The constant repetition of relationship problems and conflicts led her to define life from a negative or hostile perspective.

The decision to seek psychotherapy and continue her efforts for improvement helped her gain an understanding of her depressed moods, how to control her negative thoughts, and live her life with emotional stability. It also led her to conclude that no one, asked to be born.

Although most people do not encounter the same type of traumatic life experiences she had, there were many who reached a painful point in their lives, which led them to ask the same questions.

All of us, as living human beings find ourselves experiencing the numerous challenges of this thing called "life" without clear directions or a road map to follow.

Several case studies show how living with the mental strain of long-term stress can cause poor physical health, anxiety, depression, or suicidal thoughts.

Due to scientific research in the field of psychology, human behavior, counseling, and medications, people no longer have to live most of their lives as victim of their emotions or feel controlled by past negative experiences.

Throughout the history of mankind, there have been numerous questions, discussions, and debates about life and the realities of human existence.

It is rather common for human beings to want to know what life is, how it began, and how do we fit into the whole scheme of the human life cycle.

As complex human beings most of us spend an enormous amount of time searching for answers.

Much of my knowledge about life began as a young boy growing up in a small rural community. I frequently overheard some of my elderly neighbors say, "Live every-day as if it gon be your last, cause you don't know what tomorrow will bring or if it will come at all." A few neighbors seemed more concerned with surviving each day than about what would happen tomorrow. Some believed "no matter what happens, God will take care of it."

Starting at an early age, my family taught me to be God fearing and to believe that God created heaven, earth, and all living things. I was also taught that only God could control the natural occurrence of life, including the destiny of man. No matter what happens to you, with faith and hard work, you can still succeed in life.

As a child, I was curious about life. I questioned why God created so many different animals, especially some of the more annoying insects and terrifying reptiles.

I also wondered about the vast array of human beings, which appeared contrary to a scripture I read in the Bible about God making all men after His own image and likeness.

As a preschooler, while playing in the front yard near Mama's flower garden, I watched the different butterflies, bees, grasshoppers, and birds. I noticed how they were attracted to the beautiful foliage and blossoms of the tall sunflowers, daisies, lilies, and other plants. I also recognized how much more beautiful these flowers were planted together in the same garden than having only one type of plant to look at and admire.

A few years later, while learning how to fish, I noticed different kinds of fish swimming in the same lake, river, or pond together.

As an adolescent, I reached the conclusion that God created the world, human beings, plants, and all animals so He could admire us as His garden.

In 1959, one of my high school performances included reciting The Creation, by James Weldon Johnson (1871-1938), a poetic interpretation of how God created the world and man.

I recalled standing on stage clapping my hands, stomping my feet, and shouting "He clapped His hands, and the thunders rolled---"

I continued describing how God took a piece of clay, mold it into his own image, "Then into it he blew the breath of life. And Man became a living soul." This was the image of human creation, which I grew up with and heard repeatedly during church sermons.

Regardless of my childhood beliefs, in school, I had to learn the scientific theories about life and mankind.

In my high school biology, chemistry, and social studies classes, I was introduced to scientific studies, which indicated that life was formed in the ocean several million years ago.

While reading about the various theories on evolution and the scientific studies based on fossil evidence, I was taught that many scientists believe man evolved from one-celled organisms. I recall thinking those scientific claims were fraudulent and based on misguided information. Nevertheless, to earn a passing grade, I answered the questions according to available scientific research.

I became acquainted with the research studies of several scientists, including Charles Darwin, Thomas Malthus, and Herbert Spencer, all of whom had an early influence on the world's views about the origin of life.

Of course, on Sundays I heard a different point of view.

In school I read about the British scientist, Charles Darwin (1809-1882), who described life as "a slow process of natural selection, which evolved over many years through the passing on of heredity from generation to generation." The British economist, Thomas Malthus (1766-1834) contributed to Darwin's views about how living organisms evolved. He described life as a competitive struggle to survive for existence in a harsh world with limited resources. The British philosopher, Herbert Spencer (1820-1903), coined the phrase, "Survival of the fittest." He is widely known as a strong advocate of Darwin's theory of natural selection, which states that only the most advantaged or "well-adapted" individuals within a society will survive and reproduce. Thereby, gradually eliminating the weak, poor, and disadvantaged from the human population.

During my undergraduate and graduate years of college, I continued studying various theories about life and relationships. I also heard several speeches referring to the theories of natural selection as racist and elitist based on philosophy which some scientists used to promote racial, ethnic, and religious superiority.

In 1969, during my first semester of graduate school, I took a course in philosophy. On the first day of class, the professor asked, "Which came first, the chicken or the egg? Was it an evolution or a creation?"

Following a half hour debate and much philosophical rhetoric the class remained evenly divided between the advocates of scientific theory believing the origin of life could only be explained by biological studies of scientists, and those who argued the tenets of many religious faiths–that God is life. The professor, was interested in us knowing the difference between Plato, Aristotle, and other philosophers' views, in addition to the Christian's concept of life.

Regarding the question "What is life?" Most people's definition of *Life,* tend to reflect their individual perception based on personal or religious experiences. From a personal perspective, life encompasses all of the physical, mental, emotional, and spiritual energy experienced between birth and death. Yet even dictionaries and encyclopedias have different interpretations. I think, however, we can all agree on the widely accepted basic dictionary's definition of life, "as a condition which indicates something is alive" when it has activity, as oppose to something that is dead or inactive.

When a human being is alive, or has life, it is evident by the primary characteristics of active life or the physical functions involved, such as breathing, eating, touching, smelling, hearing, and other sensations.

The word *symbiosis* appears to be an appropriate biological term to define *life* and describe its association to the word *relationship*. For example, most marital relations results in having children. The symbiotic process of reproduction (giving life) requires a union (relationship) between a man and a woman.

According to the scientific explanation, human life begins inside a woman's Fallopian tube after her egg has been fertilized by a man's sperm. After the first few days, the fertilized egg travels from the fallopian tube to her uterus where it will be nourished—A process known as a pregnancy, which takes about nine months.

During those nine months of pregnancy this fertilized egg becomes an embryo, which develops into a human being. This symbiotic association contributes to the survival of the human species. Therefore, scientifically, it would appear there can be no relationship without life and no life without a relationship.

Scientific studies have shown that a healthy birth and survival rate of a child greatly depends on the strengths and nurturing influences of the bond between a child and a parent or caretaker. As such, a nurturing family relationship and education are two vital factors which influences the normal growth and developmental stages of human life.

During client interviews, the process for examining a person's quality of life was often measured by how well one feels about him or herself, and others, their connection to strong positive influences of nurturing relationships, and access to the resources of these connections (educational, social, religious, and financial institutions).

Education is one of the factors human beings use to enhance the quality of life, because the conditions of living as human beings between birth and death makes all of us students of life.

According to the theory of epistemology, we are born as physical and spiritual beings, therefore knowledge and information are required to nourish our humanness.

Since knowledge is empowering, many believe our education should include information about scientific research as well as the revelations of God's words.

My readings and research during my college years, included theology, psychology, and various branches of science, which helped me learn more about the theological and scientific explanations of life and human relationships.

In addition to social work, I became acquainted with:*Archaeology*—the scientific study of the remains from ancient cultures.

Developmental psychology—the scientific study of personality and behavioral changes during an individual's life span.

Social psychology—the study of how different groups behave and how individuals are affected by the rules and laws of society.

To a large extent, we have all been taught that human beings are superior to other living animals. We have been led to believe that human beings have higher intelligence and resources, which enables us to establish and shape the course of various events, conditions, and many circumstances in our lives. Yet, in spite of all of man's infinite wisdom, man can not control the various changes of the seasons, or the fundamental chemistry or physics of earth beyond pollution of the air. Neither can man control the occurrence of natural disasters—rain, flooding, earthquakes, thunder or lightning.

Including all of man's scientific discoveries, inventions, and technology, man has not been able to eliminate physical or mental illness, or defeat death.

Now, whether one believes life originated from single-celled organisms, evolved from other animals by natural selection, resulted from an explosion of chemicals flying around the universe, or created by God. No one can refute the fact that "Life," is precious, and should be viewed as a blessing by all who experience such a unique journey.

Like the scientific data being studied, personal opinions also run the gamut. It has often been said that life is a lot like playing cards—one must play the cards dealt and make the most out of the situation, no matter how difficult it appears. To play cards successfully, one must first learn the rules and develop an effective strategy. If each player is required to have a partner, he or she must learn how to adjust to each other's style and technique of playing. They have to observe each other's behavior carefully and learn how to communicate verbally and non-verbally. If they make the necessary adjustments, they have a greater chance of winning and celebrating a victory.

Yes, we all know that playing cards is just a game, and life is not a game.

Of course, life is not without it's parameters. There are standards, or rules of conduct, fair or unfairly, which society expects every individual to conform.

Increasing one's knowledge of various scientific research and information geared towards improving life. In addition to the knowledge and understanding of God's revelations about how to live a rewarding life can help every individual strive for effective and victorious relationships—friends, work, marriage, parenting, and family life.

In addition to the scientific theories, our observable life experiences have also taught us, that growth and developmental progression of human life is most often charted by our age, regardless of whether one is confronting racial, religious, or gender discrimination. Each year, or birthday, comes with a new set of rules and expectations in the life of every human being.

Experts in the field of social psychology have pointed out that conformity with these new rules and expectations ordinarily produce rewards. Such as positive attention, compliments, special privileges, job promotions, or other rewards which make a person feel accepted by others.

Studies also show that non-compliance and acts of protest to end human suffering and discrimination, also signify a healthy process of life, even though it could bring about an unfavorable response—rejection or punishment or both.

It has often been said, "Life is what you make it." and "You can be whatever you want to be in life." Yet I have never heard anyone, with conviction, say, "Life is easy." Including people who appeared to be enjoying what many described as a high quality of life.

The fact that some people have to contend with various forms of emotional and physical trauma (child abuse, racism, gender bias), and economic exploitations only makes life more complicated or stressful, in addition to the normal everyday expectations, struggles, and stress of living.

Based on experience and cases read, the quality of one's life, were most often evaluated by the difference between a person living with mental health or mental illness.

Thinking, reasoning, and making decisions are all active mental functions of healthy living human beings. These human functions and abilities are widely believed to be responsible for why so many people have been led to believe life is or can be whatever you want it to be.

Yet when some people are unable to actualize their hopes, dreams, or maintain the quality of life they desire, or live the type of life expected of them can lead to feelings of disappointment, guilt, shame, and alienation. As a result, the quality of some people's lives have been lessen by living with excessive stress, anxiety, and depression.

Millions of people have allowed their adult life to be dominated by memories of negative past experiences, which prevented them from achieving their life's goals.

The ability to imagine how life should be has made most people curious about human existence, and ambitious in their tenacious struggle for what society views as a high quality of life or the often flaunted illusion of a "good life." With the belief that there is far more to life than what meets the eye, many have amassed great wealth and materialism as a sign of a high quality of life. Leading to greed, envy, as well as social and class distinctions between human beings.

Over the years, social and class differences based on economics have led to some people thinking, believing, and being labeled as superior, while others were labeled and treated as inferior or less than human.

Such historical racial, religious, and class divisions of the human population altered the lives of millions. To a certain extent, such thinking and class division continues to provide opportunities for some to live in separate communities, attend separate schools, churches, and in some situations, work in environments with only those who share similar views and characteristics.

Living in a world with such vast array of multicultural differences, it seems unbelievable that anyone could live his or her whole life-span without interacting, communicating, or learn how to appreciate and admire the diversity and beauty of God's human garden.

In the process of assessing factors which contributes to a positive quality of life and relationships, social workers, psychologists, psychiatrists, and other mental health professionals should be cognizant of racial, social, and economic disparities.

If the success of our humanity is based on the strengths of every individual, marriage, and family life, then we should all help dispel the behavioral manifestations of prejudice. Including the distorted perspectives and pathology of racial superiority/ inferiority, which continues to influence negative attitudes, behavior, relationships, and the economic status of every living human being.

As a social worker providing individual, marriage, and family counseling, I am strongly convinced that the nature of our relationships greatly influences individual personalities and the quality of one's life.

Depending on an individual's life-span, between birth and death, research has shown how every human being transform through various growth and developmental stages of life.

After birth, every infant starts learning about conditions of life. They start breathing, eating, touching, hearing, smelling, and experiencing other sensations. Every child starts learning early in life that they must follow rules and meet certain expectations in order to grow up and be accepted in their home and community. For example, newborn infants are expected to spend most of their time sleeping. They are also expected to cry when hungry, need their diapers changed, and for other nurturing needs. Yet in most cases, following an infant's first year, even they are expected to have acquired a regular schedule for sleeping, eating, and play time.

Expectations of toddlers and preschool children are usually less restrained than the social expectations for school–aged children. An infant and toddler would be expected to wear diapers or pampers. They would not be expected to sit still and pay attention for long periods of time. Whereas, a school-aged child would be expected to be properly toilet trained and have a longer attention span.

Puberty, marks the beginning of adolescence. It is the stage of life when most individuals start getting acquainted with various characteristics of adulthood. It is also a stage of life when social and emotional adjustments are expected to be made to these new physical, biological, and psychological changes.

In most American homes, a 14 year old adolescent boy would not be expected to be self-sufficient by moving out of his parent's home and start living a life of his own, even if he did appear older than his chronological age. Whereas, a twenty-five year old man would be expected to be self-reliant.

According to many researchers, rules and expectations are suppose to serve as a model for maintaining a functioning society throughout an individual's life-span. During early adulthood, these rules and expectations quite often influence an individual's behavior and decisions about planning his/her life's goals.

A 24 year old, starting his or her first professional full time job may plan their life around the fact that they have at least 31 years before they are able to retire with a partial pension. Within the interval, between ages 24 to 55, most individuals make various decisions about marriage, parenting, health care, financial planning or investments. For some, these decisions are based on strategies for survival, including how to overcome obstacles of discriminatory practices, adjust to the emotional ebb and flow of each stage of life, while achieving age-related life goals within a specified amount of time.

Some, pattern their whole life same as their parents. In many cases, generational lifestyles have been observed in the way some people live and plan their lives, which reflects their parent's work ethics, way of managing finances, education, and relationships. Including how they cope with anger, disappointments, and stress.

As human beings grow older and reach the stage of life called middle-aged, most are confronted with a new set of life changing issues. This is a period of life when serious social, economic, and health related questions are reviewed about living beyond retirement. In addition to an assessment of how one has lived his or her life.

I know several people who live simple lives with low expectations. Some of whom never travelled outside of their hometown nor have any plans or desire to do so in the near future. For many, most of their adulthood evolved around their jobs, until they were forced into retirement.

On the other hand, some people spend most of their childhood and adult lives chasing an idea of perfection. To the point where they become obsessed with living the perfect life, without knowing exactly what is a perfect life. They spend years of useless energy trying to please others, by trying to live up to other people's expectations of who they should be or how they should live their lives.

There are numerous case studies about people who described life as a "bottomless perdition." They spend their whole life living with great distress. They feel guilty about the things they did and shameful about what others did to them.

Frequently, many also lose their way in life because they were unable to be, all things for all people.

A youthful looking 61 year old grandmother, who was a widow and retired real estate broker, enjoyed activities such as mountain climbing, skydiving, bungee jumping, dating, and dancing. She maintained an active social life, even though many expected her to live more cautiously, and participate in activities they believed more befitting of someone approaching "old age." She was motivated by a desire to live her life to the fullest. Her retirement was planned and designed to have as much fun, excitement, and adventure as possible before she became "too old," or reach the stage of life where she would be physically unable to perform many of the activities she mostly enjoy. To her closest friends, it was quite obvious she had chosen the type of life she wanted to live, in spite of, other people's opinions and expectations.

How many times have we listened to others indulge in wishful thinking or describe their fantasies about how they wish they had lived their lives, or how they wish they could make life better?

What if, life was based solely on the power of human imaginations. Would we imagine our lives as a constant source of perfect happiness and troubled free, or would we welcome the risks of new and unexpected challenges?

It is widely considered idealistic to expect a world with challenges minus the usual chaos and conflicts. But, an ideal life, nonetheless.

There are many who are blessed with the gift of life, but are afraid to live. Afraid to fall in love, marry, or have friends. They view the responsibilities of relationships as too burdensome. They are afraid to make a mistake, or be judged by others. Some live in total isolation. Beyond eating and sleeping, their lives reflect social and emotional inactivity.

Instead of active participation or interactions with others many wish for a crystal ball, which would allow them to look into the future and make the necessary changes for a perfect life. Like picking the cards you want to play from a stacked deck and never lose a game. In their crystal ball scenario, they would live a life of utopia. Everyone would be permitted to select a perfect life and not be expected to rely on his or her ability to make decisions or plan for the future. Neither would they make any of the human mistakes we all make during our life's journey.

Many of the people, I have communicated with have indicated that if given the choice they would not welcome such an imaginary or utopian scenario, nor enjoy playing cards if they had to cheat in order to win. Neither would they choose to play cards if the rules of the game were unfair and all players were not expected to play by the same set of rules and standards.

Unless, of course an individual is forced into situations which deny him or her the ability to choose how they would like to live, most people have a basic desire to live their life to the fullest and feel like winners. Everyone should have the same fundamental rights and opportunities to achieve a rewarding life.

Almost all human beings have encountered some type of negative experience which impacted their lives to a certain degree. But, as cliché as it may sound, most adults, do have choices in life. We can chose to strive for a rewarding life or we can spend life wallowing in the misery of negative thoughts about a painful past experience. We can choose to seek happiness as a way of life in the midst of life's constant bumps and grinds or we can make a conscious decision to live a life of unhappiness.

Another factor for promoting a positive quality of life involves taking personal responsibility for living a healthy and productive lifestyle—Diet, exercise, regular medical check-ups, and the type of social life one can or can not afford to live. An individual's decision to avoid overeating, drugs, alcoholic beverages, and smoking could also be a way of living a positive quality of life. Recognizing the choices one makes can influence the quality of one's life and longevity.

Most human beings want to experience a real positive quality of life (the harmony of a strong bond between life and relationships) or what many refer to as the good life—love, friends, marriage, spiritual awareness, positive parenting, and belong to a wonderful family that teaches how to live and cope with life crises.

After studying several scientific theories about life, in addition to my Christian, and professional experiences, I have learned, not everything in life can be explained scientifically.

Life, is a learning experience. Making life worthwhile is based on our efforts, choices, relationships, and spiritual awareness. As well as how we cope or survive with the human conditions that help shape our lives, including our mistakes and failures, or our triumphs, and joys.

If we are fortunate or blessed to live in a society that practices fair-play and equal justice for all, then life can be far more rewarding for every human being.

As some of the world's leading scientist continue to investigate extraterrestrial life on other planets, we mortals here on earth must learn how to work together and gain a better understanding of one another for the greater good of human existence.

Since we are unable to control or predict our future here within the universe, we should be more tenacious in our efforts to live harmoniously. We should all strive to enjoy and welcome every second, minute, hour, and day of our brief life-span as a gift and celebration of life.

My experiences have taught me that as human beings we can contribute to the directions of our destiny, even if we are unable to control it, by the choices and decisions we make, and the way we control our attitudes and behavior.

Chapter II

WHY PEOPLE BEHAVE AS THEY DO?

A ten year old child attended school frequently feeling tired, restless, and in an irritable mood.

The child's fifth grade teacher was known as a strict disciplinarian who was unaware of the child's personal problems. The teacher were coping with personal problems of their own. Twice divorced and encountering marital conflicts in a third marriage believed to be caused by unruly step-children. The teacher was believed to have a good teacher-student relationship, but like most people, the teacher also had personal feelings. There were some students whom the teacher viewed as likable and easy to teach, some were viewed as difficult and annoying, and some the teacher wished were not in the classroom.

Nevertheless, the teacher expected all of the students to be well behaved and perform up to their academic requirements.

One day this child fell asleep with their head resting on the desk. When the teacher confronted the child by tapping the child on the shoulder, the child awaken in a bit of fright with arms wailing, almost striking the teacher. Such behavior was rigidly viewed as intolerable violence by a student already marked as out of sync with the other children in the classroom.

What the teacher and the other students were not aware of, is that, In addition to a lack of proper sleep, or nutritious breakfast, the child was also being sexually abused.

For the next three years, each subsequent teacher identified this student by their record of conduct. Labeled as "the student who hit a teacher" and was treated as a student with a reputation for negative behavior.

Eventually, the child's abuser was discovered and the child was removed from the home. The child was relocated to a different high school in a different town and was assigned to a classroom whose teacher did not read the transferring records of new students, preferring to form their own opinions. This teacher was known for their established positive rapport with all students, and was both admired and respected. At the new school, this student performed exceptionally well, was respected for their conduct, and viewed as one of the top students academically.

There are many questions about the needs, drives, and motives behind people's actions and about man's inhumanity towards others.

There are also numerous theories on personality development. Many of those theories have attempted to explain how people behave while trying to satisfy different needs in a multicultural society with established rules of conduct and standards. Including information about how an individual adapt to the personal conflicts in his or her relationships.

Similar to the debate, "Which came first, the chicken or the egg?" I have also heard, repeatedly, the question, "Does attitude cause behavior, or does behavior influence attitudes?"

For the sake of clarification, lets define **attitude** as a point of view, or a way of thinking, or looking at different situations in life. Attitudes involves our beliefs and values, which are believed to be taught or learned, in most cases from experiences, (negatively or positively), and are influenced by needs and drives, which are motivated by expectations of rewards, such as a need for love, acceptance, and approval, or driven by a desire to win.

The use of the word **behavior** refers to human actions, demeanor, or how one conduct one's self under certain situations.

The term Behaviorism, is believed to have been coined in 1913, by John B. Watson (1878-1958), an American psychologist. Behavioral theories are concerned with the study of how people learn to behave, based largely on observing what people do and say during particular circumstances.

According to one theory advanced by several behavioral psychologists, "Because attitudes are deeply rooted in personality traits or unconscious mind of human beings, many people are not aware of their real attitudes. Therefore, they are prone to say one thing and mean another." Leading to the conclusion that more frequently than we realize, our behavior may reveal more accurately our attitudes of what we really think and how we really feel, than what we really say.

It is quite evident that different people have different attitudes and behaviors, but what causes some people to be judgmental, intolerant, and uncaring, when some are always trying to be impartial, patient, and compassionate?

Due to some people's proclivities for faultfinding, many think of themselves as experts at "reading" other people's conduct, based primarily on appearance, gender, or race, and believe they are always correct in their judgment.

Several case studies have shown how some individuals appear to enjoy attaching labels to categorize or describe another person or group, often without scientific data or any type of factual evidence. Such subjective labeling helps shape their beliefs, or opinions, and influence their decisions about how they will identify, treat, respond, or react towards other people.

Ask yourself, are you the type of person who feels better about yourself when putting someone down and demeaning their character? Or do you feel joyful when uplifting others and performing good deeds? Do you feel equally adaptable to assessing your own behavior as well as judging others?

In today's highly technological society, some people are so busy with the routines of their daily lives that they seldom take the time to think about what they say, do, or feel, or how what they are feeling affect their behavior or the actions of others around them.

Of course, there are those who feel overwhelmed by all of the new technology and modern day changes in marriage and family life, as well as the growing nuisance of a legalistic society. As a result, too many are living with various forms of anxieties and fear, which often control their response or reaction towards others.

The word, **anxiety** refers to feeling worried or nervous about something you think will happen. **Fear**, is an emotional or anxious feeling experienced when in real danger, pain, or confronting a disaster or stressful events.

Under certain circumstances, some of the problems and demands of everyday life can affect our attitudes and behavior by producing anxiety symptoms, such as irritability, light-headedness tension, impatience, apprehension, or worries about the future. Anxious feelings are defined as an "anxiety disorder" when these symptoms control our attitudes and behavior or interfere with our ability to interrelate sociably with others.

Lisa

At the age of 37, an intelligent, attractive, and professional woman earned her Master of Business Administration (MBA) degree, which led to the type of employment and salary of her dreams.

Due to Lisa's hard work and dedication she was promoted twice within the first three years of employment. As the new senior production manager of her department. Lisa felt anxious about going to work because she believed her co-workers despised her and did not want her to succeed. Employees socialized together during lunch breaks and occasionally after work without inviting her. Due to her supervisory position, she felt that it was her co-worker's responsibility to reach out to her. She heard rumors that several employees viewed her as aloof, selfish, and bossy.

Out of jealous envy, one of Lisa's coworkers were particularly hostile towards her and often tried to alienate Lisa from the other employees by regularly making false accusations. These rumors lead others to question Lisa's supervisory skills and integrity.

Although Lisa's work environment was stressful, she loved her job and was exceptionally conscientious of her performance. If a problem arose, she would try to resolve it, with or without support.

At the age of eight, Lisa experienced a separation anxiety following her parents' divorce, and was driven by a need to be perfect in an effort to win her parents' approval and acceptance. She graduated from high school as class valedictorian and from college with top honors. She dressed superbly, kept her apartment immaculate, and spoke with impeccable grammar. Yet she worried constantly about making her life more organized and structured. She had high expectations of herself and others, and was quite impatient with people who were disorganized, untidy, and lack respectability.

Lisa lived alone. She remained unmarried because she had been unable to meet the perfect mate or someone whom she found compatible. Although she went to church every Sunday, she did not interact with any of the church members or participate in church activities. Outside of her work and attending church services Lisa had virtually no social life. The stress on her job was causing her to struggle with insomnia, loss of appetite, and severe headaches.

It was very important to Lisa to feel accepted by others and have them view her in a positive manner. She could not think of anything she did nor what caused her co-worker to dislike her so much. She was aware of the fact that many lives and careers had been ruined because of hearsay, innuendos, rumors, and false allegations. Increasingly, Lisa was having trouble getting out of bed and going to work.

Feeling left out and ignored with no one to talk to, she worried incessantly about losing her job. The fear of failure created such intense anxiety, she initiated counseling and discovered that she was experiencing an "anxiety disorder."

During the process of introspection, analysis, and discovery, Lisa realized she could not change her coworkers' behavior, but could change her work environment by changing her attitudes and behavior.

Lisa started making an effort to establish a friendlier work relationship with her co-workers by speaking to them first and initiating casual conversation rather than waiting until they spoke. She started expressing a personal concern for her coworkers as individuals and developed an open-door policy, which led to some of her coworkers viewing her as a kind hearted and trustworthy person. By changing her behavior she observed a change in her coworkers attitudes, which led to an increase in productivity within her department and a less stressful environment.

Lisa was smart enough to know that no matter how hard she tried or how positive her response, some would continue to view her negatively. She believes it is a fact of nature that some people will not like you regardless.

There are people who prefer to think the worst about somebody else in order to feel better about themselves. Categorizing or labeling are frequently used to justify their behavior.

If some of the requirements for living a successful life are based on how well human beings get along with others and on how we should conduct ourselves in a society of rules and expectations, then we all need to learn and better understand human behavior. We need to understand how negative thoughts and feelings, whether real or imagined can influence behavior.

For example, an athlete can be the best player on the team, but if he is unable to get along with the coach and his teammates, he could easily be relegated to being a mediocre player shunned from opportunities to display his real talents.

Conflict in relationships often starts when one blames or criticize others without accepting responsibility for their own actions. It is easy to acknowledge other people's faults, short comings, and indifferent behavior. However, we all need to learn how to recognize our own internal thoughts and feelings.

Frequently, many problems in relationships could be resolved if one was able to examine how his or her way of thinking and behaving affect others.

A few years ago, I gave a talk on "Character Disorder" describing a pattern of maladaptive behavior, which becomes distorted or inflated beyond reality when some individuals encounter stress. During which time, I referred to character as a term based on "the moral and ethical qualities of human individuality," which helps distinguish one person from another.

Unresolved human conflicts appear to be as old as

mankind itself. As civilization evolved over the years, the historical clash of ideology and morality is believed to have helped men and women develop their individuality or what some refer to as "human defining qualities."

The Holy Bible and other historical documents have consistently revealed recorded information about human behavior and man's "inhumanity towards mankind." We can also read about the triumphs of righteous people who had their good reputations abused by those who labeled or described them from a negative perspective and used the power of their influence to convince others of their judgment.

It has been well recorded that Jesus Christ was not crucified because he was a bad person or "troublemaker" as was alleged during those days, but because of the people who feared his spiritual power and positive influence over Christians.

Human relationships can become distorted when an individual projects his or her feelings of inadequacies, or personal biases upon others, based on their subjective experiences.

For example, one man, described as quiet and withdrawn, felt socially inadequate in the company of others, although organizing and attending various social functions were part of his job requirements. Whenever he was asked to host a business related social event, he became anxious and worried excessively. He spent most of his energy obsessing about his performance, appearance, and about what might go wrong. He questioned whether he had planned adequately, hired a sufficient number of caterers, or if it would be successful. His nervous condition prevented him from relaxing and showing the kind of confidence his company expected of him. So, in order to relax, he would make himself a drink, then another drink, and another drink until he was the subject of the party.

As a young boy he had observed his mother plan and host numerous social gatherings for his father, which he viewed as a feminine trait. During those social events, his father spent most of his time drinking until he passed out. Because his mother was recognized as such a wonderful hostess, his father was able to maintain his job and popularity. As an adult, he had hopes of finding a wife with social skills like his mother, which would boost his career and social status in the community. Shortly after he was married, his new wife no longer wanted to attend or plan required social activities. His wife's change of behavior and his social inadequacies led to numerous arguments, mostly about what he viewed as her refusal to help his career, rather than confront his feelings of low self-esteem, alcoholism, and identity conflict.

Another example involves a woman who grew up feeling ashamed of her father and quilt about her feelings. Her father was a mechanic who struggled to support his family with erratic income from odd jobs. Inwardly, she hated him for his inability to maintain a stable job. Publicly, she often praised him and bragged about his many talents, although she felt embarrassed to be seen with him. In her confusion, she consciously believed that she loved her father and wanted a husband with similar mechanical talents. Nevertheless, she married a financial investor, who took great pleasure in playing golf and studying astronomy as a hobby, which consumed most of his free time. He grew up in a family that had a resident gardener who was responsible for maintenance of the property.

Despite their financial status, she still expected her husband to "perform the manly chores" around the house. When repairs were needed, his first thought was to hire the proper professional. He never contemplated the idea of trying to fix it himself.

Because her husband did not meet all of her expectations, they encountered numerous arguments. She never told her husband about her expectations, nor did she fully understand, at that time, why she felt so angry towards him. Since he was unaware of the reason for his wife's constant criticisms and faultfinding, most of their disputes were totally unrelated to the real issue.

Without knowing the root cause of their conflict or how to resolve it, their relationship almost ended in a divorce before they decided to seek counseling.

The honesty and effectiveness of many relationships are doomed before they start, especially when unresolved conflicts hinder one's judgment.

As a social work student in graduate school, I was taught that behavior is caused and everything we do in life as human beings has a reason, whether it is conscious or unconscious, real or imagined.

Some of the causes for human behavior stem from what many psychologists and researchers refer to as "external causes, environmental factors, or nurturing experiences."

External causes of an individual's inability to get along with others might stem from a lack of positive role models or familial support system, systemic racism, a lack of a proper education, or other needed resources required to develop a positive sense of self identity.

Other causes for human behavior are often reported to exist within the individual, which is frequently referred to as "internal causes," based on genetics, heredity, or one's nature. These internal causes of human behavior are often reported to consist of such things as instincts, drives, motives, and needs. They also consists of emotions that can affect behavior, such as love, hate, low self-esteem, and inferiority.

Several case studies have shown whether a person's

life reflect positive or negative experiences, the acquired messages or deeply rooted memories help forms their individual behavior and attitudes about life, people, and relationships. Including all aspects of love, sex, marriage, parenthood, work ethics, and religion or spirituality.

In our effort to better understand why people behave as they do, we need to understand why so many people find it easier to rely on other people's judgment.

It often appears as though some people prefer to pre-judge others before establishing all of the facts. Some base their opinions on what they have heard other people say, rather than trust their own internal feelings, observation, or on how that person relates to them.

During an interview for a new job in a new town, Tina described herself as naive and impressionable, but one who works well with others and easy to get along with.

On Tina's first day at work, a disgruntle employee warned her about different cliques and personalities of coworkers. This employee suggested whom Tina should communicate with and whom she should avoid.

In her effort to fit-in and feel accepted, Tina trusted her new coworker's judgment and heeded her warnings. A few weeks later, Tina was embroiled in office politics—a personality conflict with another worker, which led to her resignation.The disgruntle employee whose judgmental persuasion contributed to Tina's dismissal, remained on the job and did not offer Tina any further advice or support. Instead, she avoided Tina, as though she were persona non grata as soon as she heard about the new employee being accused of showing favoritism among coworkers and causing inter-office conflicts.

One man reported that he once dated the girl of his dreams, but she failed to pass his 'buddy connection' test. During the date, he found her to be very charming, fun to be with, and an honest person. He was excited about the prospects of their next date. After he introduced her to his "Buddies," he was ridiculed about her "small breasts and homely" appearance, so he decided not to telephone her for another date. About three weeks later, he saw one of his "buddies" out on a date with the same woman. About nine months later, he received an invitation to their wedding. After listening to repeated conversations from his "old buddy" about what a wonderful, trustworthy, and loving wife she was, he realized what he had lost by not trusting his internal feelings or instincts.

We also need to know why so many people experience low self-esteem, jealousy, and envy.

Another example, of how low self-esteem, jealousy, envy, and negative attitudes can lead to conflict at work, lets examine the situation between Ian and Luigi.

Ian, an electronics engineer, was hired by a small, family owned manufacturing company, which exports computer hardware and software to foreign countries.

After the company started importing parts at low discounts, their production and sales increased. Then, they were able to start hiring new employees.

This was Ian's second professional job since graduating from computer training school. He was excited about his status as a rookie. He liked the attention he regularly received from his co-workers who were always friendly and helpful. In addition to the camaraderie, he was also paid an excellent salary. Seven months later, the company hired Luigi, a computer software designer. He was also well received by all of the other employees, except Ian. For some unknown reason, Ian simply did not like Luigi, even before they were properly introduced.

Luigi was gregarious and extremely competent in his job duties, but Ian refused to make an effort to get along with Luigi, and avoided communicating with him, unless it was strictly job related.

Eventually, Luigi detected that he was not well liked by Ian. The other employees also sensed the tension between Ian and Luigi, which was out of character for a company that thrived on its reputation for maintaining a positive work environment. The company attributed it's growing success to good employee relations, performance, support services, and employee discounts.

One day, Luigi offered Ian the schematic for an important program design. In Ian's usual abrupt manner of trying to disregard Luigi, he told him to just put them on his desk. Three months later, when the company was expected to sell the software programs to their subsidiaries as part of a multi-million dollar project, it was discovered that Ian had never looked at the specs. Not only did the company lose several millions of dollars, but had scarred its relationship with valuable partners.

Luigi grew up in a loving family that taught him about unconditional love. He had always felt loved by his parents and three siblings for who he was and not for his performance or career status. He was never made to feel pressured into becoming anything other than what he wanted to be in life.

Ian, on the other hand, was an only child, reared by two high powered career parents who were never able to share much time with him during his childhood. His father wanted him to become a lawyer. His mother wanted him to become an artist. Neither, ever made him feel loved or as a priority in their lives. Ian, spent most of his childhood in private schools, and his summer vacations at summer camp. Most holidays were spent visiting different relatives. He grew up believing that the people who cared most about him were those who made him feel like he was the center of their undivided attention.

Ian, nor his co-workers were aware of the fact that his attitude was responsible for his mood swings and inability to get along with others when he was not the center of their attention.

We also need to know why one individual will react to certain situations one way and another person respond in a totally different manner to a similar situation. For example, why would one man in an overcrowded bar accept an apology from a man who accidentally stepped on his foot, and another man would rather punch the man out than accept an apology.

Several authors have reported that an individual's attitude about a particular experience or situation most often determines his or her inclination to react or respond.

Stephen

A 21 year old, five feet, six inches tall, muscular built man who frequently visited bars and night clubs on Thursday, Friday, and Saturday searching for lonely women whom he could manipulate into a one night sexual rendezvous. He was not interested in developing a commitment or long-term relationship. To him, marriage was for squares and losers. Stephen did not express any remorse or guilt about his exploitation of women. Even when he met a "nice girl" who would express her affection and a desire to develop a romantic relationship with him, he would reject her after he was able to "score" have his first affair with her.

An ostentatious attitude of friendliness in a man was viewed as a definite sign of weakness, which Stephen refused to exhibit, even for a pretty woman. He firmly believed that displaying a rough demeanor was a sure sign of masculinity.

One night, while nursing a bottle of beer and scanning the crowded dance floor, a man accidentally stepped on Stephen's foot. Although the man quickly apologized, Stephen pushed the man and punched him in the face.

This incident could have turned into a vicious fight had the club's bouncer not stepped in between them as quickly as he did to restrain them and avert further actions.

Stephen was escorted out of the club while cursing and swearing his revenge. The other man, brushed himself off, asked the bouncer, "What's wrong with that guy?"

As a baby, it was not unusual for Stephen to be spanked, left alone all day with an unchanged diaper, or cry himself to sleep. He grew up in a family where the pattern of relationship was based on parental authority and "a child knowing his place," conformity. In his house, physical punishment was regularly used as a means of discipline and to exert control.

Stephen was born the second child of five siblings. Each of his siblings had a different father, who had lived with their mother until she became pregnant. None of the fathers made any significant contribution towards the care and rearing of their child.

Stephen's mother was an angry and depressed woman who repeatedly talked about her scorn towards "no good men who ain't nothing, but dogs."

While growing up, Stephen and his brothers frequently heard their mother say, "no one can trust a man." Yet shortly after she was abandoned by one man, another man would be permitted to move in with her and the children. She was also an alcoholic who consistently attracted men who shared her passion for drinking. They showed no interest, nor took the time to be nurturing. The children were often viewed as unwanted responsibilities, who had to learn at an early age to take care of themselves. Most days, between Monday and Friday, Steven's only meal would be a free lunch at school.

It was not unusual for Stephen or his brothers to see their mother and one of her boyfriends sleeping during the middle of the day following their almost daily binges.

Stephen was seven years old when his mother's latest boyfriend moved into their apartment. His mother's boyfriend insisted that the children call him "Mr. Jean" instead of "Dad" as they were instructed during previous relationships. Mr. Jean was a tall, muscular built man, who was emotionally and physically aggressive with the children. Mr. Jean was allowed to punish Stephen and his brothers physically and verbally. Their mother seemed pleased to relinquish her parental control.

During the few rare occasions he was sober and in a "good mood" he might give the children "a little spending money," while constantly reminding them he was not their father. During many of his drunken tirades he would brag about being the man of the house and tell the children how ungrateful they are about having a man in the house to take care of them.

At the age of eight, Stephen was recognized as a withdrawn, but kind and gentle young boy, who expressed an interest in reading and learning. Frequently, Mr. Jean referred to Stephen as a "little sissy" and told him and his brothers they would grow up to be a "bunch of punks" unless they start acting "tough, like men." He said, "Being a man mean standing up for yourself and not taking any [crap] from nobody."

Stephen and his family lived in the poorest section of a large inner city, where the high school drop-out rate, drugs, and crime were high. His wiry body and sensitive nature, made him the object of neighborhood bullies. Twice a week, Stephen participated in an after-school computer learning program for kids. One day, after his extracurricular activity, he was attacked by two older boys who were brothers. They beat him, then dragged him into an alley. While the younger brother held him down, the older brother raped him. After he was able to stop crying, he walked home, but was too embarrassed and ashamed to tell anyone about his molestation. The next week, one of the molesters tried to attack him again, but Stephen ran home sweating and trembling as he announced that a boy, known as the neighborhood bully had taken his book bag and was chasing him. Mr. Jean took off his belt, beat Stephen and put him outside. He told him not to come back until he get his bag and beat the boy up.

Subsequently, Stephen's demeanor changed, he started dressing like he was a member of a street gang, using profanity as though it had replaced the English language, and became involved in numerous fights. He was expelled from school for beating up another student and taking the boy's lunch money.

By age 11, Stephen had developed a serious conduct disorder. His delinquent behavior and increasingly explosive personality caused him to be labeled an incorrigible child. By the age of 14 his name was well known within the juvenile court system, but consistent efforts were made by a juvenile probation officer to keep him in school.

An appointment was scheduled for Stephen to talk to a psychiatrist, but he failed to appear.

The probation officer also tried to encourage Stephen to participate in youth activities or community programs that would promote positive self-esteem and skill development, all to no avail.

Following several suspensions and being expelled from school, Stephen was transferred to an alternative education program, which he refused. No one in his family made an effort to encourage him to improve his behavior or stay in school. He dropped out of school at the age of 16.

Based on Stephen's family life and the environment he was growing up in, there did not appear to be any expectations he would succeed in life. His thoughts were consistent with the belief that no one liked him or cared about him. He did not believe in prayers or turning the other cheek. Christian and moral principles were not part of his childhood upbringing. No one had ever taken him to Sunday school nor had he ever attended a church service.

No one had ever engaged Stephen in a mutual exchange or negotiation that respected his feelings. Because he had not developed a meaningful personal relationship with anyone, he adopted the attitude that he did not care about his life or the life of others. His attitude made it difficult for him to relate to other people, especially authority figures. Including his probation officer, who made several attempts to help, by attending his court hearings, serving as an advocate, and offering alternative solutions to keep Stephen out of jail. The probation officer also tried to communicate with Stephen and convey his concerns for Stephen's welfare, but each attempt was met with resistance. In addition to Stephen's inability to carry on a civil conversation, trust was also a major factor. Other than his probation officer, Stephen had never known anyone who was willing to help him without demanding something greater in return, which made it hard for him to trust his probation officer or anyone else.

By the age of 17, Stephen had developed a hostile and defiant personality. His rage was motivated by a psychological need for revenge. He started behaving as if he did not have a conscience. He was extremely sensitive and almost always in an angry mood. If someone looked at him in a way that he interpreted as a "dirty look," or in a manner he believed questioned his masculinity, was immediately perceived as a threat or a challenge, and a cause for a fight, even if the other person had no idea why he was being attacked. A complicated question or simple criticism could easily provoke Stephen's rage and become a reason for a fight.

Instead of trying to settle a dispute by talking or reasoning, fighting appeared to be his only solution.

Six months after the bar room incident, Stephen was
arrested for second-degree attempted murder (threatening with a gun, although no shots were fired), second-
degree kidnapping, and assault during an armed robbery
of a grocery store. He was sentenced to prison for 30
years.

While in prison, he was examined by a psychiatrist
and received a battery of tests by a psychologist.
Stephen's diagnosis indicated he had a psychosis, based
on a pattern of distorted reality with his thinking, behavior,
and seemingly lack of empathy with others. His treatment
included taking medications for poor impulse control,
especially for his compulsive sex drives, which was
believed to be responsible for his violent behavior.

Stephen was encouraged to talk to a priest and a
Muslim minister who volunteered as prison's chaplains.
The minister had a reputation as a father figure to many
of the young prison inmates. He was able to persuade
Stephen to start reading and participate in anger manage-
ment group meetings. In addition to his rapport with a
Muslim minister, Stephen also received psychiatric and
christian counseling.

For the first time in his life, Stephen was forced to
examine his own attitudes and behavior. After describing
his childhood during a group session, one of the inmates
confronted Stephen. He said:

"Hey man, sounds like life dealt you a bad hand,
but look, all of us here have issues which caused
us to end up in this place. The key is, you got to
learn how to turn all that [crap] around if you
expect to survive in here or out there."

After several years of counseling and confrontations,
Stephen recognized that life had dealt him a bad hand

and he had lots of reasons to be angry. But as an adult, he has a choice and the responsibility to decide whether to continue his self-destructive behavior or learn how to live without the anger. He also realized that although he had made many mistakes, bad decisions, and choices, he was amenable to change. He needed to develop mature ways of negotiating and managing his life, if he has any hopes of getting out of prison and living a productive life.

In prison, Stephen earned a high school diploma, and after eighteen years, a college degree. At the age of 45, after serving 23 years, he was scheduled for a clemency hearing to request a parole.

Tyrone

Tyrone was a six feet, three inches tall, popular and charismatic young man. After graduating from high school, at the age of 17, he entered a technical training school and became a licensed electrician. After completing his training and apprenticeship, he was hired by the city's electric company. After reaching the age of 21 with a regular income, he decided to locate an apartment and move out of his parent's house. He wanted to become self-sufficient.

Tyrone decided to celebrate his independence with a few close friends who helped him move. One of his closest friends was his first cousin, Bob, who recommended a local sports bar for beer and catching up on the latest sports news.

It was a Saturday evening, and the bar was over crowded, so Tyrone and his buddies decided to leave and go to a restaurant near by for a steak dinner instead. On their way out of the bar, a man accidentally stepped on Tyrone's foot, which almost tripped him over. The man quickly apologized. Tyrone, immediately accepted the man's apology and said, "No harm was done." Both men, walked away without any thoughts of violence.

Before moving into his new apartment, Tyrone lived with his parents, grandfather, younger sister, and brother. His grandfather was a retired postal employee who moved in with Tyrone's parents shortly after the death of his wife. Tyrone felt close to his grandfather and appreciated having two positive male role models whom he could consult for personal advice and direction.

During their childhood, Tyrone and his siblings had to attend Sunday school and church services every Sunday with their parents who were actively involved in various church activities. He was also encouraged to participate in sports, but had to concentrate on his academics as a priority. Yet he did play two years of varsity football.

Tyrone grew up observing his father treat his mother and siblings with respect. His father actively participated in the rearing of his children and attended all family functions. Seldom, if ever, did his parents miss one of his extracurricular school activities. He credited both parents with teaching him how to respect them, himself, and the rights of others.

Tyrone's attitude about life and people, as well as how to control his behavior came from observing how his parents and other members of his extended family conducted themselves.

He also watched his parents set goals and achieve them. At least once a month, his parents sat at the kitchen table writing out checks to pay bills and plan the family's budget. In Tyrone's house, a new situation, planning a vacation, or a family crisis was always a cause for a family discussion.

In addition to his parents, Tyrone had several other positive role models from his community, school, and church. These influences helped him develop a positive outlook on life and self confidence.

At the age of 21, Tyrone was still dating the same girl that he escorted to his senior class prom, Taneisha, who was one year younger. After Taneisha graduated from high school, she entered college to become a pharmacist. Taneisha had one more year before she was scheduled to graduate with her degree. During her visit home for Thanksgiving, Tyrone asked her to marry him. She said, "Yes!" Their engagement was announced during the Thanksgiving dinner, which included both families. Wedding plans were scheduled for exactly one year from the date Taneisha was scheduled to receive her degree. They believed the two-year engagement would allow them sufficient time to plan, save, and mature, for a successful marriage and family life.

Numerous studies on child development and human behavior indicate that attitudes and behaviors of parents towards their children clearly influence patterns of childhood development.

Terms such as "needs, motives, drives, and instincts," are frequently used by scientists and researchers to explain why human beings behave as they do. In an effort to clarify the use of these terms, which are frequently being used in this book, let's define them thusly:

Needs—In psychology, needs are based on our body's physical, emotional, and psychological requirements to grow and sustain life. Our human needs are what cause us to develop drives, motives, or an urge to perform specific functions. Although most people experience a variety of emotions or feelings, such as love, joy, sadness, anger, fear, or hate. Some of our basic human emotional needs includes a need for love, affection, pleasure, happiness, and attention. In his hierarchy of human needs, American psychologist Abraham Maslow (1908-1970) identified needs for love, security, and the attainment of goals as important as the need for food.

Motives, refer to desires, emotions, or reasons which stimulate humans to act in a certain way in order to fulfill a particular need, purpose, or goal in life. For example, the reasons why many people go to work everyday are to establish and maintain a career, pay bills, accomplish goals, and take care of their families. Motives for eating breakfast before leaving for work could be to avoid hunger pangs or provide the body with required nutrients in order to maintain a healthy lifestyle.

Many case studies reveal how most human beings are motivated by expectations of rewards—acceptance, appreciation, friendship, popularity, job promotion, a rewarding life, and most frequently, for love.

Drives—In psychology, drives are human urges aroused by a physiological need or thought, which stimulates a strong or intense desire to be satisfied. All human beings have the same basic physiological need for food, water, air, sleep, elimination, and shelter. For example, hunger is one of the drives which reflects the body's physiological need for food, same as feeling thirsty creates a strong urge or drive to drink, or a bloated stomach for elimination. The drives to fulfill these needs are required to prevent starvation and for human survival. Our human emotional drives reflect the nature of our thoughts, feelings, desires, or passion. Some people are driven by an urge for personal gratification— a desire for success and recognition, or pleasure and sex, or peace and harmony. Instead of planning long-range goals, some seek immediate gratification as a way to satisfy their strong urges or drives.

Basically, the biological, physiological, or emotional changes in the human body causes a need to arise. Such as hunger, thirst, or a sexual drive. These needs, in turn, arouses a desire or motive. The motive produces an action or a series of behavioral responses.

Instincts, are believed to be responsible for behavior patterns developed from (heredity) one's parents. Many genetic and biological studies seem to indicate that heredity is responsible for all human actions, feelings, and thoughts. That human beings are born with biological characteristics and a certain predisposition, which are not always affected or altered by cultural, or external influences. Once again, stirring the debate between "nature versus nurture."

The debates appear endless. There are also studies that do not believe that instincts adequately explains why human beings behave as they do, without studying the external factors occurring in an individual's life.

A few have advocated—the process of learning how to behave starts after conception. Some believe that the process of learning how to behave starts immediately after birth with the belief that conditions of life requires all human beings to adjust to their unique environmental circumstances.

The English philosopher, John Locke (1632-1704) is recognized as one of the earlier contributors of child development research. He advanced the theory that a newborn infant enters into the world without an inherited predisposition, but with a clear lack of knowledge that is gradually shaped by experiences.

The French philosopher Jean Jacques Rousseau (1712-1778), another earlier contributor to the field of child development, argued that "heredity" guides every aspect of child development and human behavior.

It is well known that during the transition of healthy newborn infants, from life in their mother's womb, to the world outside, they have to start the process of learning. They must immediately start breathing, adapt to a different climate, start eating, and the process of elimination. A child's ability to process information and interact with his/her new surroundings is widely believed to help shape their intellectual, social, emotional, physical, growth and development.

We know that a newborn will instinctively start feeding to satisfy their hunger needs. They will also respond to the stimulation of touch and sound. We also know that at a very early age, children start learning how to let their caretakers know what their needs are, and when they need it.

When most infants feel distressed—alone, frighten, wet, hungry, or in pain, some will soothe their discomfort by crying, or by sucking on their finger, or both.

Of course, in most cases, crying is often an infant's signal for help. Under circumstances that many view as normal, the infant will be picked up, examined, and have their needs met by a nurturing guardian.

According to the child development research done by American psychologist Mary Ainsworth, a baby's formation of an emotional bond or "attachment" to its primary care giver is an important development. Especially during the infant and toddler stages, which includes the first three years of life.

It appears that most researchers and mental health practitioners agree that patterns of development, attitudes, and behaviors are determined by the interaction of both "Nature (internal) and nurture (external)."

Many, agree with the premise that a child that grows through his/her infant, toddler, childhood stages having their basic physiological needs met. In addition to their needs for love, stimulation, having their diaper changed regularly by an attentive and nurturing caregiver are more likely to develop a pattern for positive behavior and the ability to get along with others.

I have known several people who grew up feeling ignored, neglected, abandoned, and unloved. In many cases, they described themselves, their environment, and other people from a negative perspective. Some of these individuals had learned how to seek other ways to meet their unmet needs during childhood, such as throwing temper tantrums, engaging in risky and attention getting activities, or were involved in delinquent activities.

Several case studies have described how emotional deprivation can stunt a child's physical and psychological growth.

There were cases, which indicated that depending on the duration and intensity of early emotional deprivation, some children died or became emotionally injured for the rest of their lives. Even after they become adults and were able to develop some type of loving relationship.

History has taught us that in some cultures during the time of rugged individualism when children grew up under difficult circumstances, many developed survival skills which enabled them to become more successful than their parents or the previous generation.

The question is, whether a child growing up under difficult circumstances will be strong emotionally, socially, physically, and intellectually.

During the early years of American life, known as the days of rugged individualism, before social security, retirement pension plans, or child welfare laws, when many families survived by living off the land and were forced to make do without modern conveniences. Many survived eating fruits and vegetable grown on their land. Due to hunting and fishing they were seldom without meat. An over abundance of crops harvested or animals farmed or hunted led to bartering for money or store bought items from neighbors who had access to transportation. They fetched water from the wells they dug, and learned how to live without electricity, refrigeration, or telephones. During a drought or famine, it was not unusual for families to be hungry, nor was it unusual for parents to leave small children at home with older siblings. Life was rough and crude, yet many viewed their way of life as economically sufficient, with the belief that they had control over their lives.

In 2003, we were inundated with news reports about a two-year-old female toddler who survived after being left alone in her mother's apartment for nearly three weeks.

According to several news reports, the child survived by eating "raw pasta, mustard and ketchup." After the child was taken to the hospital, where she was examined and treated for malnutrition, various television stations, radios, and newspapers reported that a hospital spokesman revealed that the toddler was "doing well" and that she was "talking and laughing with the nurses."

As many people gasped from the various news reporting the toddler's heroic survival, I think most, if not everyone felt relieved to hear that the child had survived and was "doing well." Nevertheless, we must ask ourselves, what about the thousands of other children not discovered in time, that do not survive. And the children who are discovered abandoned and abused, what about the repercussions or long-term effect?

We do know, however, that despite one's childhood experiences, the choices and decisions made, as well as how a person behaves in his or her adult life, most often determines the quality of his or her life and relationships.

In most cases, very few people are concerned about an adult criminal's childhood, or what caused a person to do bad things, or why some people consistently make the wrong decisions.

Some case studies reveal how individuals who develop a negative self-image, as a result of being rejected by a biological parent or guardian may unconsciously seek out situations or people who will continue to reject them. Thereby, creating a cyclical pattern of relationship conflicts.

Jane

A young woman in her early thirties said that she spent her entire childhood visiting doctors regarding complaints of one illness after another. Although none of her medical examinations revealed the source of her physical illness, she was, nevertheless, treated for asthma. She also spent a large portion of her grade school years visiting the school's social worker for disorderly conduct.

After four failed marriages, Jane found the help she needed and started on a career path that changed her life.

During counseling, she discovered that while growing up with her two siblings, she was her parents least favored child. She could not recall either of her parents relating to her with the same admiration and attention accorded to her younger sister, Kimberly, or her brother, Billy.

Her involvement in psychotherapy during her early adulthood years also revealed that much of her childhood illnesses and disruptive classroom activities became a way of forcing her parents and other adults to play an active role in her life.

Jane grew up in a family that had the outward appearance of a stable and happy family life, but to Jane, her family's dysfunction were hidden behind closed doors.

Jane's parents were of German ancestry. Her father, Mr. Gebauer, was compliant, unassertive, and an alcoholic refrigerator repairman who spent most of his time outside of the home. He seldom participated in family discussions or activities. Jane's mother, Mrs. Gebauer, was a homemaker who was left in charge of all decisions regarding managing the house and child-rearing. Mrs.

Gebauer was described as an overbearing and controlling woman who constantly criticized and disparaged Jane and her father. Mrs. Gebauer accused Mr. Gebauer of not being a good provider and an inept companion. Jane believed her father stayed away from home to avoid her mother, and because she could not recall ever having a conversation with her father, she wondered if he was also avoiding her as well.

Jane was nearly two years older than Kimberly, and almost three years older than Billy.

It was well known, inside the family's circle that Mr. Gebauer had always wanted a son. He was frequently overheard saying, "The day Wilheim "Billy" Gebauer, Jr. was born, was the happiest day of my life."

At the age of 16, Billy was six feet, and weighed over 250 pounds. In high school, he was an average student and a mediocre athlete, but his father treated him like he was a hero. No matter how hard Mr. Gebauer worked or how much time he spent outside of the home, he never missed any of Billy's school activities.

Jane could not recall her father ever attending any of her extracurricular activities or showing any type of interest in her life.

Throughout Jane's childhood, her relationship with her parents remained distant and strained. Based mainly on rejection, criticism, control, and anger. For the most part, Jane felt ignored and unwanted. All of her efforts to search for a sense of individual identity or assert her self-determination were most often rejected by her mother, ignored by her father, and overshadowed by Kimberly and Billy's activities.

At birth, Kimberly was given the name Heidi Kilm Gebauer. On her 13th birthday she insisted every family member call her Kimberly because most of her school-mates called her Kimberly since first grade, and she believed, more befitting of her personality.

Although she appeared to be anorexic, Kimberly was an honor student and popular cheer leader who participated in several beauty pageants. Unlike Jane who was overweight, clumsy, and withdrawn. Kimberly adored her doting mother who treated her like a close friend rather a daughter. She was allowed the freedom of self-expression and encouraged to participate in various activities which helped her explore her talents and social skills.

Jane could not recall her mother ever criticizing Kimberly, but remembered that she regularly sided with Kimberly during their sibling rivalries.

Frequently, Jane stood by, listening to her mother compliment Kimberly, or watch them go shopping together without inviting her.

Jane's decision to sign-up for the school's soccer and volley ball team was harshly criticized by her mother as unladylike. Her mother said that sports would make her appear as a tomboy, which did not fit the image she had planned for her daughter.

Following several attempts and failures to lose weigh so she could qualify for one of the local beauty pageants, Jane signed up for the school's band, but was rejected.

While experiencing a sense of hopelessness in her efforts to gain her parent's approval and acceptance, Jane gave up. She simply stopped trying, adopted a negative attitude, and started a pattern of self-recrimination. Her deep feelings of failure, low self-esteem, shame, and anger led to complaints of illnesses.

After Jane adopted the belief that she could not do anything right. She started believing she was a failure and not worthy of love.

Jane was a very lonely young girl who felt alienated from her family due to what she described as a lack of affection or emotional support. She also felt isolated at school where she was viewed as a loner, even though she tried desperately to make friends.

In her effort to seek attention and acceptance, Jane tried hard to please others. Occasionally, she would embarrass herself while trying to be a crowd pleaser.

Her classmates avoided any type of association with her outside of the classroom. They thought she was "too needy," emotionally. Their brief interaction with Jane at school were spent listening to her personal problems and complaints.

For the remainder of Jane's high school years, she engaged in various self-destructive activities. She smoked, drank beer, and were promiscuous with boys who were eager to offer her attention away from school, in private.

Immediately after graduating from high school, Jane, at 18, married the first man that expressed an interest in marrying her. She thought that moving out of her parent's home would bring her instant happiness and freedom.

Shortly after the wedding, Jane discovered that her 33 year-old husband's personality resembled that of her mother's pattern of rejection, criticism, and control. Their marriage was void of love, trust, honesty, and mutual respect.

For nearly a year, Jane tried to maintain her loveless marriage while coping with her husband's controlling and abusive behavior. She was unable to find any comfort from her mother who insisted that she should be happy to have someone who wanted her.

Even though Jane viewed herself as an adult who no longer lived with her parents, her mother still found it difficult to compliment her, use words of acceptance, or tell Jane that she loved her. Her mother regularly told others that she loved Jane, Kimberly, and Billy—all the same. Yet most of Jane's visits with her mother were spent listening to repetitive complaints about how Jane should live her life or about the things Jane did wrong during her childhood.

As an adult, Jane still yearned for a closer relationship or some type of an emotional bond with her mother, but with each attempt she felt thwarted in her efforts.

Most of Jane's visits with her family left her feeling like a misfit, or something was terribly wrong with her, and that she still could not do anything right.

Jane thought about seeking counseling to discuss her personal and marital difficulties, but decided against it because she was afraid her involvement in counseling would be interpreted as failure, as an adult, same as her childhood. She continued feeling isolated and alone, until she had to seek medical attention for a venereal disease, which she contracted from her husband who frequently flaunted his many extra-marital affairs. It was then that she decided to file for a divorce.

Living alone for the first time in her life, Jane decided to attend college part-time while employed as a proof reader at a local newspaper company. Although she had hopes of becoming a child psychologist, she allowed her self-doubts to deter her from her goals. She took courses in arts and literature.

At the age of 19, Jane had matured and developed a sexually appealing body. She relished the overt attention that she frequently received in public from so many different men. Due to her low self-esteem, she began dressing very provocatively in public—wearing seductive clothing that revealed her physical attributes, but demeaned her character. Her obsequious behavior often led to several indecent advances from men she viewed as undesirable and dangerous. Nevertheless, she felt excited by their attention.

Nine months after Jane's divorce, she started dating

one of the college administrators on campus, a 42 year old married man who left his wife and children to marry her.

Jane's second marriage was based on distrust and suspicion. Neither trusted the other, and both suspected the other of being unfaithful during the other's absence. Beyond the physical aspects of their relationship, they did not have anything in common. Jane's second husband divorced her and returned to his first wife. Her second marriage also lasted less than one year.

Jane became involved in an interracial relationship. Two years after her second divorce, she entered her third marriage, which caused her parents to disown her and refused to permit visits to their home with her new husband who was black. He was born in Nigeria, spent most of his childhood in Jamaica, before moving to America. He was described as the strong silent type who never complained or criticized her. She believed that he loved her and wanted to make her happy, but due to her low self-esteem and believing that she was unworthy of love, she found it difficult to accept his affection.Nevertheless, she married him because she enjoyed his company and the unparalleled attention he provided.

Following years of constant criticism and rejection from others in her past, she had learned to believe that she was too defective for anyone to ever truly love her. Unable to separate the reality of her past from her current situation, Jane adopted her mother's behavior and became overly critical and demanding of her husband, as though she were trying to force him to reject her. Although, Jane was becoming increasingly critical of her husband, their marriage had been far less stressful than any of her previous relationships. From Jane's point of view, her husband's calm demeanor and lack of spon-taneity, resembled her father's absence and rejection.

Prior to their wedding, Jane's husband spent every Friday evening after work playing dominoes with his "Island friends," and soccer on Sundays, which he continued to do after their wedding, with Jane's approval. As Jane became more critical and demanding, she insisted that he share his weekends with her, which he agreed to do outwardly, to keep the peace in his marriage. Inwardly, he harbored resentment towards Jane for forcing him to give up what he viewed as his greatest joy outside of his marriage.

The irony of their situation—the more time they shared together, the more their relationship deteriorated, until their divorce.

By the age of 24, Jane had been married and divorced three times. After her third divorce, she became involved in numerous sexual relationships. Her heavy drinking and other self-destructive behavior led to her using drugs.

At the age of 27, Jane married a 35 year old man named Hans, whom she had been sharing an apartment with for nearly a year, and who was providing her with a regular supply of marijuana. Hans had never been married, but was the father of five children by three different women. He was unemployed and did not assume any financial responsibility for any of his children. Jane supported her husband and his drug addiction.

In high school, Hans was a starting quarterback for the football team and a very popular athlete, until he was kicked off the team and expelled from school for selling drugs and steroids to other athletes and students. After his brief incarceration he seemed unable to adjust to life without the notoriety of football and the euphoric feelings of constantly having fans follow him around like idol worshippers. Without football, he viewed himself as nothing and nobody. His daily use of drugs and alcohol was a form of self-medication, which he believed, or hoped would help him forget the painful memories of what once was his glory days to never be recaptured.

Hans met Jane at the Staats–Zeitung newspaper company where she was employed. He had accepted employment there as stipulated by conditions of his probation. He quit as soon as his probation ended and returned to selling drugs.

Because Hans came from a similar Germanic background as Jane's parents, Jane was once again invited to her parent's home for visits, with Hans. Although, Jane did not reveal the nature of his social and family history.

This was Jane's fourth marriage and the most contentious. Hans was unfaithful and often treated her with contempt, but she was in denial and pretended not to notice. He preferred to spend most of his time in their apartment only when Jane was away, or at work. Otherwise, he was in the streets, selling drugs, and getting high with his new friends who reveled in the nostalgia of yesteryear.

The little time Hans and Jane shared together mostly involved using drugs or fighting. Their communication was limited to Hans shouting profanities or calling her names. Because denial had become her way of coping, she seldom reacted to his tantrums. Instead, Jane appeared content, as long as he continued supplying her with drugs. It appeared as though Jane was accepting their dysfunctional relationship as normal behavior with the belief that she did not deserve anything better. In addition to her other problems, she was also addicted to drugs.

Four months after their wedding, Jane arrived home from work and found Hans in their bed with another woman. They were both dead. According to the coroner's report Hans and the other woman died from an overdose of diluted narcotics.

The trauma of Jane's discovery led to hospitalization, drug treatment, and several years of psychotherapy.

Part of Jane's treatment involved family therapy and consultation with her parents.

During which time, Jane discovered that she was an adopted child.

Before Jane was adopted, Mrs. Gebauer was told she could not bear children after her third miscarriage. The news was painfully received, so she and Mr. Gebauer decided to adopt. They wanted a male infant with fair skin, blue eyes, and blond hair, but white male babies were greatly in demand and rarely available. The only child that came close to meeting the other characteristics of their choice was a six month old baby girl named Jane. Within a few months after the adoption, Mrs. Gebauer became pregnant with Kimberly. Eleven months after Kimberly was born, she gave birth to her son, Billy.

After Mrs. Gebauer gave her husband a son, and she had the type of daughter she had always dreamed of in Kimberly, there did not appear to be much time, energy, or attention left for Jane.

During the beginning of the scheduled four family therapy sessions, Mr. Gebauer sat quietly and only briefly answered questions asked of him. For the first time, Jane heard stories about his ancestral past. Mr. gebauer was the youngest child of five offsprings born in Germany. He grew up listening to stories about Germany, Hitler's regime, and how his grandfather was killed in an October 1917 battle. After Germany loss the Battle of Versailles, most of his family fled Germany to escape persecution. They loss contact with one another during the relocation as many were scattered throughout different parts of Europe. His father, a member of the National Socialist German Workers' Party and a soldier in the Nazi army stayed in Germany until the invasion of Germany in1945. His real family's name, which he refused to give to the therapist was changed while living in Eastern Europe.

In 1948 The Displaced Persons Act made general provisions for the immigration of thousands of displaced immigrants in Eastern Europe including displaced Germans to the United States of America where they were immediately provided with food, clothing, shelter, employment counseling, loans, and assistance with small business development.

One of the results of Mr. Gebauer family's influence on his attitudes, is that he never developed a tolerance for racial diversity. He viewed all non-caucasians and Jews as inferior or criminals.

Mrs. Gebauer was allowed to do most of the talking. She described herself as a Christian and how she had always blamed Jane for the rift in their mother/daughter relationship. "Jane was always moody and an onerous child." She said.

Towards the end of the therapy sessions, Mrs. Gebauer said she was not aware of Jane's feelings until she started attending the family therapy sessions. She called Jane a liar and child who pretended to be sick just for attention. She did not apologize, nor did she ask Jane for forgiveness.

Although Mrs. Gebauer showed no remorse for her behavior or any empathy for Jane's feelings, the therapy sessions did allow both to talk freely and share their feelings with one another. This was the first time Jane felt confident enough to confront her mother and father with her personal pain and feelings.

The therapy sessions helped Jane change her way of thinking about herself, family, and life in general. By changing her thoughts, Jane changed her life.

Following her father and mother's revelation, Jane decided to take ownership and responsibility for her own life. Everyday, after waking up, she would think of something positive and plan her day around her positive thoughts.

Jane spent the next seven years rebuilding her life. She returned to college, graduated, and became a licensed school psychologist.

Chapter III

ON LOVE AND SEX

Imagine, if you will, two strangers, a 38 year old male college professor and a 29 year old female concert pianist, meeting for the very first time, in an art gallery. An Australian sculpture caught their eyes simultaneously while perusing what had been advertised as a spectacular art collection. The sculpture, became a conversation piece, and an opportunity to politely make comments about the artist's extraordinary attention to details. An art print by Salvador Dali "Person at The Window," also led to mutual appreciation. While admiring the painting by Dali, their comments turned into a casual conversation about surrealism and the influence of Dadaism on the early 20th century art movement. They were both college educated and single. After discovering that they both shared a mutual interest in classical music, poetry, and other fine arts, led to an invitation to continue the discussion over dinner. Followed by a night cap at a local bar. After exchanging telephone numbers and addresses, they agreed on the time and place for their next date.

Not unlike many couples, while becoming acquainted, their conversations focused more on their mutual interest in arts and hobbies, rather than about life and relationships.

Immediately following their first sexual liaison. The college professor started viewing their relationship as a commitment. He felt exuberant about finally meeting someone whom he believed to be compatible, socially, intellectually, and sexually. Three months after their first date he started making plans for a joint future—shopping for an engagement ring and a proposal of marriage.

Despite the fact that she had enjoyed the professor's company, she was not interested in developing a long-term relationship, at least, not at that time. Her career, which required extensive traveling, took priority in her life, and she viewed sex as "a pleasurable experience that can be shared and enjoyed with the person of your choice."

The professor, who had spent years searching for a stable relationship was disappointed and experienced the emotional pains of an unrequited love affair.

Throughout history, men and women have been attracted to one another for various reasons. For many, sex is usually the first attraction. Whether one choose a mate as a sex partner because of sexual characteristics, or for marriage and reproduction, or because he or she believed it was true love at first sight, sex, almost always play a major role in people's perception of compatibility.

Relationships form significant connections between human beings, but can be complicated. Yet there are many who prefer to remain confused by their new lover or spouse's real intentions rather than ask that one big mysterious question—"Is it love or just good sex?"

Most individuals involved in romantic relationships want to know the answer, but are afraid to ask because they are not sure if there is a difference between love and sex. And if there is, they are uncertain about what it is. For many years, I have also searched for an answer to the question—What is the difference between love and sex?

After studying history in high school and college, it was evident that before the historical moral crusades, reformation movement, and rise of Christianity, the meaning of love, sex, and marriage were quite different from the modern day 21st century beliefs of romantic love and monogamous relationships. Even the King James' version of the Bible include scriptures about love and sex.

I have heard several debates about Adam, Eve, and the "forbidden fruit," and many express surprise after reading "The Song of Solomon," or learn that the Bible contain several verses about sex and sexual matters. Some believe that issues pertaining to sex are too controversial to be written in the Bible. Others have argued that it is very appropriate because love and sex is a necessary symbiosis for maintaining life and humanity.

In the religious education course I studied in 1964 at Edward Waters College in Jacksonville, Florida. The class included information about three Greek words for love: **Eros**, sexual love or desire; **Philia**, friendship or brotherly love; and **Agape**, Christian love. For this chapter, I will add the fourth Greek word for love—***Storge***, parental love and affection.

1. Eros, a term which generally refers to romantic or sexual love, from which derives the Greek term *erotikos* "erotic" referring to something sexy or sexually arousing.

In Greek literature, Eros was known as the "god of love." He was also worshiped as a fertility god. According to Greek mythology, Eros was the son of Aphrodite, "the goddess of love and beauty," from whom the Greek word "aphrodisiakos," aphrodisiac is derived, which means to "induce sexual love."

2. Philia, from the Greek word, *philios*, "to love." A word used to denote genuine affection. Philia was frequently used to describe friendship or brotherly love, as reflected in the name Philadelphia (city of brotherly love). In human relationships, philia reflects the type of love between close friends who mutually experience genuine feelings of liking, fondness, and affection, as well as share a specific kind of loyalty and respect for each other.

3. Storge, is a Greek word used to describe parental love or the love between family members. A storge type of love is believed to be instinctual and unconditional. Based

on the premise that you should love your sister, brother, mother, father, husband, wife, son, or daughter despite his or her imperfections, faults, or mistakes. An example most often used to describe storge love, is the maternal love of a mother for her newborn baby. This philosophy includes the belief that a mother and father should also love their son and daughter for who he or she is, not for what he or she can accomplish.

4. *Agape*, from the Greek word "Agaph", meaning "love." In earlier days, the word *agape* was used by Christians as a reference to their "love feast" in celebration of the Lord's Supper.

Modern day usage of the word *agape* refers to "Charity" or "Christian love." The type of love that is non-sexual, spiritual, selfless, and unconditional as exemplified in God's love for humanity, or Christian love—the kind of love every human being should have for one another.

The term "unconditional love" means exactly what the words imply, real, pure, or true love without conditions, restrictions, or limitations.

Several psychologists often describe the term "unconditional love" as a pattern of behavior or relationship that exists or should exist between a parent and child. Yet it seems that many adults are constantly seeking a relationship with another adult who will love them unconditionally.

Unfortunately, too many people are disillusioned about the difference between love and sex. Consequently, far too many relationships end with disappointments due to unrealistic expectations, or because they often confuse performance and desire for immediate gratification with true love. Many, still question, whether it is humanly possible for human beings to love another person other than God, unconditionally.

One of my favorite scriptures in the Bible, which describes agape love, is known as the "Gospel of Love," found in First Corinthians, 13th chapter:

"Love is patient, love is kind. Love is not jealous, it does not appear phony or deceitful. Love is not snobbish or condescending. It is not rude, it is not self-seeking, it is not prone to anger; it does not hold grudges. Love does not delight in evil but rejoices with the truth. It always protects, always trusts, always hopes, always perseveres. Love never fails."

Unlike the first three Greek words for love (Eros, Philia, and Storge), agape or spiritual love is believed to be the highest form of love, because agape love is based on God's love, which is eternal.

Beyond the Christian concepts of love, I found that many authors equated "love" with "sex." The American Heritage Dictionary of the English Language (1971), defined love as, "An intense affectionate concern for another person." and as "An intense sexual desire for another person." Some writers believe that romantic encounters or falling in love was by fate or destiny, and some believed it occurs only accidentally or as a result of mutual self-interest.

In the 60s and 70s, reading was my primary source of information for answers on the topic of sex and love. Some of the materials I scrutinized considered sex and love to be an equal complex emotion. A few authors and philosophers focused on the question "If we can have love with or without sex, then why can we not justifiably have sex with or without love?"

In an attempt to define love, various writers, poets, scientists, and philosophers have described love as a physiological function caused by sexual arousal. Some interpreted the word love as an euphemism or label used to define a human emotion caused by a strong sexual attraction towards the opposite sex. Many of these beliefs, led to the premise that the word love was used primarily to characterize intense romantic involvement and to justify a commitment in a monogamous relationship.

The ability for human beings to love oneself and others has long been recognized by researchers, psychologists, and other mental health workers as a fundamental concept and basis for mental health. The inability to love or express feelings of affection has been interpreted as one way of assessing mental illness.

Some researchers have attempted to prove that the ability to love stems from basic human drives and motives, based on an established system of reward and punishment. For example, the ability to love and be loved often reap the rewards of fulfilling human needs for a sense of belonging, feeling attached, and bonding with others. The ability to love and be loved can also result in pleasant feelings, romantic events, or shared memories. An inability to love or feel loved, often leads to low self-esteem, loneliness, alienation, and isolation.

Occasionally, I heard someone say, "I'm looking for love," or "searching for the love of my life." Much too frequently, their search resulted in experiencing a sexual relationship without the symbiotic benefits of mutual love.

As a young college student, I wondered, silently, of course, how does anyone learn the difference between love and sex, or about life and relationships.

With so many confusing definitions about love, I also wanted to know how a person would know when he or she has found love, true love, or real love, and how would one determine whether that love is reciprocated. For me, that question appeared to be one that only life experiences could answer.

After graduate school, I was hired as a social worker, providing marriage and family counseling, which motivated me to continue reading more extensively.

It was during my professional career that I started gaining a clearer understanding of the scientific theories about the role hormones play in stimulating sexual behavior and how our minds send messages throughout our bodies, which stimulate sexual urges and desires.

Learning about the various parts and functions of the brain was fascinating. The brain coordinates and controls our metabolism and other bodily functions. In addition to the way we think, breathe, talk, walk, see, hear, taste, how we respond to emotional situations, and our sex drives. The brain is made up of billions of nerve cells acting as a human communication system, transmitting messages between one another, known as neurotransmitters, which is able to store, retrieve, and interpret these messages.

My research led to information that indicated that sex and sexual activities had been studied since ancient history. The *Kama Sutra*, written in India in the second century BC was recognized as one of the best known ancient manuals on love and sexual performance. It contained information about the spiritual aspects of sexuality with illustrations of several positions and techniques for enhancing sexual pleasure.

The scientific study of human sexuality began in Europe and the United States during the nineteenth century Victorian Age, which has been described as a time of repressive sexual standards and behavior in comparison to the described promiscuous behavior of some of the earlier generations.

It is well documented that Sigmund Freud, founder of psychiatry and psychoanalysis considered sexuality central to his psychoanalytic theory. His method of treatment with neurotic patients involved his search for insights into the human personality. Of course, his ideas were considered controversial.

According to Freud's writings, he believed that the essentials of personality development started in early childhood. He was sharply criticized for considering sex a major force in human behavior and for insisting that sex drives first appear during infancy.

Freud's writings also suggested that sex was the core of most (male and female) human problems. He recalled how as a young boy he had lust for his mother and hatred for his father. He believed that sons wanted to kill their fathers and take their place, and that women suffered from "penis envy." Many rejected Freud's theories of psychoanalysis as unscientific and some referred to his works on sexuality as "pornographic writings."

Nowadays, the internet, television, books, and several magazines provides easy assess to information, demonstrations and illustrations about sex. Occasionally, the topic of love can be heard in a song, church sermon, or read in a romance novel. It appears as though the accessibility of pornography greatly overshadows the availability of any structured sex education courses. I think the most damaging effect that pornography has on our present day society is the negative images it portrays of women, its focus on immediate gratification, and the tremendous influence it has on so many curious young males and females. For this reason, if for no other, there should be stronger efforts to plan and organize structured sex education courses that teach healthy principles about love, sex, and male/female relationships.

Have you ever wondered why so many movies are produced about sex and violence than movies about love and peace. Have you ever listened to the intensity of a discussion on the topic of sex, compared to a discussion on love? It has often been observed that whenever one ask a question about love, almost inevitably, the conversation gravitates toward a discussion about sex.

In 1973, the Family Service Association of America(FSAA) Tri-Regional Practice Institute sponsored a full week of several family life education workshops in Pocono, Pennsylvania, which I attended as a marriage and family counselor. Towards the end of the week, I attended the "wrap-up session" of a course on "Dealing With Sexual Dysfunction." After listening to a lecture on the techniques modified from the works of William H. Masters and Virginia Johnson, I decided to attend the film segment part of the workshop scheduled for later that evening. The film segment covered several subjects on the topic of "Sexual Behavior-Treatment Modalities." The 13 short documentary films were explicit and illustrated various sexual expressions, positions, and treatment methods for many different types of human sexual problems.

According to the course information brochure, the primary objective was "to sensitize participants to the range of human sexual expression; provide the practitioner with a greater understanding of their role in this problem area; and develop beginning intervention skills as marriage and family counselors."

As a young social worker, I watched those films with utter amazement and provided my full attention to every minute detail. It was distracting when some of the participants laughed out loud. Many were snickering and giggling like school aged youngsters. I did not want to miss any aspect of that opportunity to learn as much as possible about sex. Up to that point in my life, I had very little knowledge about the subject, beyond my limited reading about scientific theories, and personal experiences, which was not sufficient enough to use as a frame of reference for professional counseling.

I had not read or seen anything that could parallel those films, which illustrated the physiology of sexual

functions, autoerotism, human fantasies, massage therapy, premature-ejaculation, frigidity, and impotence. There
was also a film about the importance of effective verbal
and non-verbal communication skills.

The more knowledge I gained about the physiological
functions of the human body, the less inhibited I felt about
discussing sex and sexual behavior, especially with
clients in marriage counseling sessions. The knowledge
and ability to use correct terminology were great assets in
helping clients understand how their psychology and
physiology related to their sexuality or sexual dysfunction.

The experience gained from the workshop in the
Poconos, added with my clinical social work skills, helped
me feel more competent to manage my marriage counseling case assignments.

A couple, in their mid-thirties who had known each
other since high school were married after the husband
was drafted into the military.

During their separation, while the husband was on
military duty overseas, he became involved in several
sexual affairs with prostitutes. He did not consider his
behavior as being unfaithful to his wife, because he
believed that his sexual activities were "just financial
transactions with prostitutes to relieve tension." After his
active duty in the military ended, he told his wife about his
experiences, with the belief that it would "encourage her
to become a better lover," and help him maintain an erec-
tion during their diminished sexual activities.

The wife viewed her husband's behavior as "vulgar,
unfaithful, and dishonest." She was struggling with issues
of trust and anger, which caused her to retreat rather than
feel closer to him or make any attempts to satisfy his sexual desires. She described him as insensitive. He complained that she treated sex like it was dirty.

Their dilemma and lack of effective communication

created a great deal of tension and conflict, with increasing arguments about seeking a divorce.

Regular weekly counseling sessions were scheduled. During the initial conjoint sessions, whenever the word "sex" was mentioned, the wife would wince. I informed her of my observation. She said that she had been reared by strict parents who were Christian fundamentalists. She was taught that sex (without using the actual word) was taboo and that engaging in sex beyond reproductive purposes in marriage was an act of the devil. She was adamant in her belief that the different sexual activities her husband wanted her to perform were "perverted and sinful."

The husband was quite graphic and descriptive with the details of their sexual relationship.

I requested their permission to substitute the word "sex" with "making love" when referring to that aspect of their marriage relationship during the counseling session. They agreed, but the wife continued to flinch. At one point, when her husband was describing his "needs," she cringed and covered her face with her hands.

Both were encouraged to talk about their childhood experiences, relationships with parents, teachers, peers, religious education, and others that influenced their attitudes and behavior about love and the physical act of making love. It appeared that their attitudes towards love and sex were quite similar before the husband's military experience with prostitutes, which he believed accelerated his sexual drives and fantasies. The husband acknowledged that after returning home from Vietnam, he was more demanding with his wife whom he blamed for his bouts of erectile dysfunction. His behavior reflected his insensitivity towards his wife's distrust, feelings of inadequacy, and low self-esteem.

While focusing on the learning and conditioning of

their sexual behavior, they were encouraged to practice effective communication skills. This process involved positive reinforcement by using complimentary language rather than words that would impede the opportunity for each to listen or talk without being interrupted, as well as various exercises leading towards resolving issues of trust, commitment, and forgiveness.

After a few weekly counseling sessions, the husband started responding to his wife's feelings and needs. He acknowledged his wife's right to refuse to participate in any sexual activity that makes her feel uncomfortable. He also started accepting responsibility for his behavior.

The husband acknowledged that his anxiety about his future after leaving the military, in addition to his intense feelings of guilt about violating his marital vows, his obsessive anticipation of his wife's rejection, and fear of losing his wife were the causes of his impotence.

During a very touching moment in the session, the husband sat facing his wife, with tears in his eyes as he held her hands. He apologized for using her as a scapegoat for his fears and personal problems. He asked his wife for forgiveness and promised to remain faithful. He also told her that she was the first and only woman that he has ever been in love with, and that he cherished the life they shared together.

Following a few more weekly sessions, the issue of love and trust became less of a topic for discussion. Both indicated that they were very much in love and wanted their marriage to last. I observed the wife responding as though she felt less intimidated. She participated more actively in the discussions and appeared more at ease expressing her feelings and needs. She started using words and phrases like "making love, sexual activity, playing around, and sex." She acknowledged that the counseling sessions had helped her realize that love, trust, commitment, and the ability to communicate should take priority in a marriage. She wanted to trust her husband again, and was willing to give him a second chance. She also wanted to stop feeling guilty and ashamed of her own repressed sexual desires, and was looking forward to share varied experiences with her husband.

Evidence of her growing confidence was when she sat facing her husband and described her sexual needs. She told him that she also has sexual fantasies, which causes her to feel sinful, guilty, and ashamed about the fact that she could entertain such thoughts. But, mostly, she has a recurring desire for him to just hold her. She described her need for them to share intimacy by holding each other in an emotional embrace, nurturing each other while touching and kissing. "Ocassionally, I need to be caressed, without completing the physical act of sex or intercourse." She said.

As part of a process to enable them to learn how to communicate more effectively, I shared a magazine article regarding the work of Masters and Johnson on the topic of sexual behavior in marriage. The magazine was loaned to them with a request that they read and discuss the article together. I also requested that they be prepared to share their opinions about the article during the next scheduled session.

Both the husband and wife shared information about how counseling had helped them learn more about themselves, each other, and how to communicate feelings that neither had revealed previously. Now, they were more knowledgeable about the difference between just having sex and emotional intimacy.

The technique of assigning "homework" proved to be an effective tool. I recognized that for each subsequent scheduled session, the couple arrived at the office holding hands, smiling, and touching more freely during their conversations, as though they had fallen in love, all over again.

The last scheduled session was used to discuss the process of case termination. Both thanked me vigorously for "saving" their marriage and strengthening their lives. I recalled telling them that it was their love and commitment for each other that motivated them to save their marriage.

Sexual activity in a marriage relationship, especially among couples who are in love with each other, is often referred to as "love making," or "making love" and can be intensely pleasurable, physically and emotionally. The key ingredient is "mutual love."

A few years later, as part of my on-going research, I attended a workshop on sex in Westport, Connecticut. This was a very frank, explicit, and mature workshop on sexuality and communication.

A few months later, I conducted two seminars on the topic of " sexual communication" in the conference room of my private practice office located on Wall Street in Norwalk, Connecticut. The participates were asked to define "love" and "sex". Approximately 21 out of 24 men and women defined sex as an "act," and love as an "emotional feeling and a commitment." A few defined sex as a "physical act of love when it is not violent or coerced." Some described sex as a "marital obligation," performed for reproduction and marital pleasure. One person said they did not believe in love and described sex as "a carnal act that can be performed with anyone at anytime."

If a relationship is based solely on sex, one must ask, what happens when a partner loses his or her sex drive, sexual appeal, or their internal sex organs no longer function adequately to meet the other partner's sexual satisfaction. Is the decision to remain together considered fulfilling a commitment or is it an act of love?

Many people, think the word "celibacy" only refers to

unmarried individuals practicing abstinence from sexual activity, or as a form of religious asceticism. There are many married people suffering from impotence, frigidity, and other sexual dysfunction caused by a physical or mental disability. Some, thought their sexual disability were permanent, but after a referral for a complete medical examination, and accepting counseling, they discovered that their dysfunction stemmed from a psychological condition. It was also revealed that a temporary disruption of sexual functions may result following surgery, or from use of necessary medications.

When a sexual dysfunction occurs in a relationship, married couples are confronted with the question, "Is love able to conquer all and sustain the relationship, or does the healthy spouse leave the relationship for another healthy partner?" Such a question often begs another question, "Was the relationship based on mutual love or good sex?"

It seems that one could assume that the shame, embarrassment, and "hush-hush" nature about discussing sex and sexuality have contributed to many individuals suffering alone, in silence, needlessly. There have been various sex related disorders, diseases, and complications which were treatable. Some, possibly, curable if the condition had been detected in it's earliest stage.

Despite the controversy, sexuality is a part of life, which includes the physical and psychological development of human beings, as well as their moral or religious beliefs. Human sexuality also help shape our culture, behavior, and attitudes as it relates to various life issues. Such as gender, relationships, sexual activity, choices about parenting, and child-rearing.

There are many that believe that sexually transmitted diseases are the primary concerns of people under the age of thirty, and that impotence and frigidity are primary concerns of men and women over thirty. Of course, there are numerous studies to confirm this belief, however, people need to know that age, alone, does not prevent you from exposure, or contracting venereal diseases. Personal responsibility must be practiced by all ages.

Interviews with couples struggling with various sexual problems revealed that age was not always a deterrent for sexual dysfunction. Pre-mature ejaculation, impotence, or erectile dysfunction were major complaints for several men, young and old. Dryness, painful irritation, loss of sexual desire, lack of physical arousal, and their spouse's inattentiveness were chief complaints among many women. These problems could occur at any age, due to physical or psychological reasons.

There were several young people trying to cope in marriages void of sexual activities due to an automobile accident, obesity, alcoholism, drug addiction, emotional distress, or some type of mental illness.

In many cases, psychotherapy and physical fitness have helped people improved their mental and physical health. As well as increased their libido or sex drives.

A few couples appeared surprised to learn that some of their sexual problems concerning arousal and performance could be ameliorated with more kindness and patience. By caressing, kissing, talking or "pillow talk," saying "sweet nothings," and simply, being nice to one another before, during, and after sexual activity. The most essential ingredient, however, is based on mutual love and trust.

It has often been said that love is a subject most men prefer to avoid discussing and sex is a predominantly male preoccupation. That is not an accurate description. Both, men and women, have very strong sexual drives, and both are capable of uncontrollable sexual urges.

There are many males and females who recognize

that a mature romantic relationship should be based on the spiritual, emotional, and physical aspects of love rather than solely on sex. Nevertheless, there are many men and women who remain confused about the difference between love and sex.

Admittedly, a large number of men still believes that talking about love is "too mushy," and talking about sex is manly. In one case, a man preferred to buy his wife expensive gifts and flowers rather than use the four letter word, "L-O-V-E." When his wife complained that he never tells her that he loves her, he purchased more gifts and a greeting card inscribed with the words, "I love you!"

In general, many of the human relationship conflicts between males and females center around misguided information about the difference between love and sex.

From a sociological point of view, if all human beings were taught at an early age how to differentiate between love and sex, I think we would all enjoy a more positive and healthier relationships.

Numerous stories have been heard from people who said they never had a conversation about sex until they became an adult. Some did not become aware of the difference between love and sex until after encountering emotional trauma or a relationship problems. In many cases, these relationship problems resulted from a lack of knowledge about sexual feelings or biological changes occurring in their bodies, which were mistaken for love. Some described how they confused infatuation, obsession, and fantasy with what they thought were feelings of love.

There are males and females who said they had never experienced emotional or spiritual feelings of love and felt incapable of expressing what they thought most people viewed as love. Some had only experienced the physical act of love, therefore believed that having sex was the only way they could express their love.

Several research and case analysis indicate that certain attitudes about healthy or unhealthy relationships are formed during childhood. For many, the confusion about love resulted from their conflict or trauma stemming from incest, rape, or from observing the behavior of their parents or other adults that influenced their lives.

Yalda, a very attractive 32 year old woman who resembled the type of woman most men would find both physically and sexually appealing. She had smooth skin, lustrous hair, perky breasts, slim waist, well proportioned hips, and full lips. She described herself as an average looking woman with low self-esteem. She seemed unaware of her flirtatious smile and demeanor, which was her way of compensating for her low opinions of herself. She described how she had fallen in love with a different man almost every weekend since she was 20 years old. She enjoyed the company of men, the anticipation, sexual arousal, and the euphoric feelings during sexual activities. The feelings of passion which she had experienced were described as love, although she would quickly lose interest immediately afterwards and feel bored until her next relationship.

Yalda did not understand nor could she identify her feelings or strong desire for sex with so many different men. She wanted to change her behavior, but felt powerless to stop or control the constant surge of sexual desires, which she described as overwhelming.

A nervous break down at the age of 30, and a desire to maintain a commitment to one person in a relationship forced her into psychiatric treatment.

From age 12 to 20, she was sexually abused by her mother's live-in boyfriend, Raul, whom she said had also been sexually abused when he was a young boy.

Raul was unemployed and emotionally immature with

a reputation as a "lady's man." He was nine years younger than Yalda's mother, Carmen, and 12 years older than Yalda.

Due to his childish behavior, Raul acted and looked much younger than his chronological age. According to Yalda, most people thought she looked older than her age. Her physical development and appearance had brought about several rapid bodily changes. By the age of 12, Yalda was already menstruating and had developed a mature woman's body. Often, she felt the same age, and sometimes older than Raul.

Yet despite Yalda's physical growth, her mental, emotional, and intellectual development continued on the level of a 12 year old child.

Due to Carmen's long working hours, Yalda, as an only child was often at home alone and had to assume several responsibilities. In addition to the usual household chores, Yalda had to do the cooking, house cleaning, and laundry. Yalda, also had to make her own preparations to get to and from school, discipline herself to study and complete homework assignments. When Carmen was not at home Yalda was not permitted to go outside to play with her peers, she had to learn how to entertain herself.

As a single parent with an hectic schedule, Carmen tried to divide her weekend spare time between her daughter and Raul. Initially, she would only agree to see Raul late evenings after Yalda was asleep. When Yalda became 12 and was viewed as mature for her age, Carmen believed Yalda was old enough to understand her mother's need for male companionship. Carmen started inviting Raul to her house for regular visits, until he moved in as Carmen's roommate.

Frequently, during their family's outing, Raul was very playful with Yalda, without any suspicion from Carmen, who found his behavior amusing. Yalda enjoyed the time she shared with her mother and Raul, but became aware that Raul was more playful with her during Carmen's absence. Raul's playfulness led to lightly touching, kissing, and fondling. Yalda, interpreted his behavior as being affectionate, although she did not understand the powerful feelings and emotions being aroused.

Eventually, Raul provided Yalda with a lot of time and attention while teaching her how to please him sexually. Yalda became infatuated with Raul, and after experiencing her first intercourse, she believed it was love.

Yalda was 16, when Carmen and Raul broke up and he moved out of their home, but the sexual abuse, which she described as a loving relationship, continued regularly on weekends for four more years. She learned how to manipulate her time and schedule so she could visit Raul on weekends without her mother knowing her whereabouts. Throughout high school, she missed practically all of her weekend class activities, her prom, and part of her graduation activities just to be with Raul. After high school she continued her weekend relationship with Raul, until he moved in with another woman, an older woman who was financially able to support him.

At the age of 20, Yalda was still a very lonely young woman who did not have any close emotional ties to anyone in her family nor any close friends. She felt rejected and devastated when Raul ended their affair and moved in with the other woman. She described their separation as the most painful experience of her life, which unknowingly, caused her to enter a deep depression. To prevent her mother from discovering her secret, Yalda refused to talk to anyone about her problems. She blamed herself for her predicament while living with guilt, shame, and anger.

For the next ten years of her life, while searching for love, each weekend, sex became a substitute for meeting her needs for an emotional relationship. Because of her insatiable and compulsive desire to have sex with so many different men, some of the men she dated called her a nymphomaniac.

Those numerous unfulfilling sexual activities contributed to the severity of her depression and low self-esteem until her nervous break down and admission into a psychiatric institution.

Following a few months of in-patient psychiatric treatment and medication, she was referred to a rape crisis center for on-going counseling. During her recovery, she became aware of the emotional, mental, verbal, and physical aspects of child abuse. She discovered that some of the symptoms of sexual abuse during childhood could cause an addiction to sex, guilt, anger, isolation and loneliness, depression, anxiety and fear, trust issues, poor self-image, and dysfunctional relationships. She also started learning about the difference between love, sex, and rape.

In another case study, a young couple in their early twenties initiated marriage counseling regarding a lack of trust and sexual frustration. The request was based on the wife's complaints about the husband's refusal to have sex unless it was at night, in bed, under the cover, and with all the lights turned off.

The husband's explanation was that he loved his wife, but could only perform in the dark.

They attended several conjoint sessions of marital conflict exploration, until the husband requested an individual session. He apologized to the counselor for his lack of candor. He had deliberately withheld information about his childhood experiences while his wife was present. He revealed that when he was a teenager he arrived home early from school due to an illness and saw his mother in bed with a stranger while his father was at work. His

mother made him promise to never tell his father or anyone about what he had witnessed.

This occurred at a very crucial stage of a 14 year old
male adolescent whose mind and body was experiencing
various hormonal changes. In addition to his increasing
curiosity and fantasies about the opposite sex.
Subsequently, every time he saw or thought about a girl
in the nude, he was reminded of his mother and haunted
by his oath of silence and betrayal.

His feelings of guilt interfered with the close relationship he had with his father and his ability to continue communicating openly and honestly. He became angry and
distrustful of others. His confusion led to emotional conflicts, which he internalized.

Due to his ongoing anxiety about discussing his
secret with his wife or anyone else, it was now interfering
with his marital relationship.

After sharing his revelation, he described a feeling of
relief. Counseling helped him develop a positive perspective about his existing love for his wife and his ability to
trust her as the unique person she was.

Following a few more individual and joint sessions he
felt confident enough to share his secret with his wife. He
gained the understanding that he and his wife were
accountable for each other and not for the mistakes of
others. With his wife's support and encouragement, he
developed the ability to express his trust and admiration
during the day or night with the lights on without experiencing a traumatic episode.

Sexual and physical abuse affect all children, male or
female, whether it is caused by incest, rape, or premature
sexual involvement.

Everyone, needs to learn the difference between love
and sex. In addition to promoting healthier relationships,
such knowledge could also help reduce the increasing

number of children and adults who become victims of various sexual deviant behavior.

In modern times, it has always appeared easier for women to discuss their feelings and emotions about painful love relationships. Today, in the midst of changing cultural views towards the role of traditional men versus modern men, there are still men who find it extremely difficult to talk about love, feelings of sadness, grief, or emotional trauma. Whether it involves physical or sexual abuse as a young boy, or coping with feelings of rejection as an adult, some men, almost inevitably, indulge in self destructive behavior, instead of talk about their feelings.

It has also been observed that almost as many men as women experience depression and other emotional crises following the breakup of a romantic relationship. In many cases, whether it is the male or female, studies reveal, the one that ended the relationship for another partner often described less emotional conflict, adjust, and moved on with his or her life.

Historically, many men have expressed their feelings about love in various forms of literature, history books, poetry, and songs. There are numerous stories and some have been told or written by men about the hardships of falling in and out of love several times before finding the "right person" or real or true love, or a "soul-mate."

One such story, is about a man, twice divorced, but married and involved with two other women. His first wife divorced him after she fell in love with another man. After witnessing his second wife's infidelity, he had a panic attack. When asked why two mistresses, he replied, "In case one leaves me, I'll have another." When asked what would happened if all three leave, he said, "I'll get three more."

In his counseling sessions, he acknowledged his first wife as his first true love, and their divorce, as the most painful event of his life. His second wife was someone he had known and trusted since childhood. Although he loved his third wife, he acknowledged that he was harboring deeply rooted anger towards his first two wives.

His involvement in counseling led him to realize that his need to maintain two sexual relationships outside of his marriage served as a defense mechanism against the pain he was experiencing. His actions was prolonging his insecurities and distrust, which prevented him from fulfilling his commitment of loyalty and trust to his third wife. His behavior also prevented him from realizing and accepting the type of intimacy and love he desired from his wife.

Today, in our modern society, the subject of sex and love are no longer as well-hidden or considered taboo, or only written about by poets, songwriters, and research scientists. It appears that in this new millennium of 2000, almost everyone has an opinion about love and sex, and most seem willing to talk or write about their views and experiences. Yet there still appears to be a tremendous amount of confusion about the difference between love and sex.

There are literally, millions of articles, essays, memoirs, and other written materials by people describing their romantic or sexual involvements as "love affairs."

I have heard several stories and read numerous books and articles about people "falling in love" with a married person who later rejected them and renewed their relationship with their spouse. These emotional ordeals resulting from the rejected person's experience were often described as an "unrequited love affair." Leaving one to ponder whether it was love or sex.

Increasingly, many popular books are being written, describing women as more emotionally involved when it focus on the subject of love and marriage, and men continues to be described as more interested in the physical aspects of a relationship.

Fame and fortune have resulted from the writings of many authors about the "exploitative nature" of love and sex. And there are still many authors who inscribe the belief that sex should be freely performed and enjoyed without love, but love can not exist without sex.

Over the years, my interviews with couples married for more than fifty years who still expressed feelings of affection and abiding love for their spouse, even though, in many cases, sexual activities had diminished or ceased due to physical or medical conditions, have demonstrated to me, a few lessons about the meaning of true love.

A husband, who remained faithful, loyal, and attentive to his wife for 43 years after she underwent a double mastectomy in the ninth year of their marriage, and several other surgeries, which left her infertile. At their 52nd wedding anniversary he described his wife as the, "Love of my life."

An attractive, healthy, and youthful looking 57 year old wife remained chaste and unaffected by the frequent stares and invitations from younger men, even after her 70-year-old husband suffered a stroke and was not able to perform in the satisfactory manner they had always enjoyed.

Most people learn to expect that a parent's love and Christian love are and should be unconditional. As human beings mature from childhood to adulthood they must also learn how to love themselves in addition to their parents and others.

My life experiences have taught me to believe that by the very nature of all living human beings, love, which is an emotional, spiritual, physical, and religious experience, is as much required for human existence as air, water, food, clothing, and shelter. Sex, which is based on a human physiological and emotional need should be an affectionate expression of true love and for the purpose of reproduction in order to continue mankind.

In a romantic or marital relationship, love should be a shared experience between a man and a woman, which produce feelings of togetherness and mutual self-fulfillment. Love should also be about caring and sharing, freely and completely, above and beyond one's selfish interest, without either feeling victimized or exploited.

Love, like sex, is a strong and powerful feeling. When true love or real love, is reciprocated emotionally, spiritually, and physically, most people will recognize it, not just in their loins, but in the very nature of their brain, heart, and soul.

First and foremost, in order for anyone to recognize real love, I believe in the premise that everyone must first learn to love him or herself before they are capable of loving anyone else. Secondly, I believe that in a romantic or marital relationship, true love must be mutual in order to be real.

Only through knowing who you are and understanding others, will you be able to determine whether you are in love, infatuated, or just sexually aroused.

Chapter IV

14 NOTES ON MARRIAGE

Long-term marital relationship has often been viewed as one of the most gratifying aspects of life.

Historically, the institution of marriage has undergone several changes. In some cultures, polygyny was considered acceptable and legitimate. In many other cultures, monogamy was recognized as the acceptable and legal standards of society. In some cultures, the selection of a spouse was outside of the bride and groom's control due to an arranged marriage. Nevertheless, in most cultures, the state of matrimony has long been viewed as a sacred bond.

As early as the 13th century, marriage was accepted as one of the seven sacraments—a symbol of the unity of Christ and the church.

In earlier times, most monogamous marriages remained intact and tried to fulfill the marriage vows—"Until death do us part."

For many, marriage became the basis for forming a family, which was primarily responsible for child-rearing, and for that reason, most marriages tried to remain intact.

Today, there are many reasons why people enter marriage. Motives vary according to individual beliefs, needs, desires, lifestyles, and available resources. Some women and men believes that when they reach a certain age, their body clocks start winding down, especially around the age of "thirty-something." Such beliefs often trigger anxiety and a rush to marry, which could lead to settling for a partner that may or may not be compatible, or starting a dysfunctional relationship.

Some believe it is better to marry, even after their intuition convince them that the risk of getting a divorce appears evident.

It is not uncommon to hear or read about people who marry to gain financial wealth, improve their social status, or due to pregnancy . News about high divorce rates are currently focusing on the increasing number of immigrants who deceptively marry Americans to acquire residential rights or citizenship.

Ideally, we would all like to believe that most people marry for love, and their love will help maintain a happy marriage and family life.

Couples considering marriage would be well advised to attend a pre-marital preparation and marriage planning workshop. They should also make serious use of their time by asking and answering the following questions:

a). What are your reason(s) for getting married?

b). What are your views on marriage, family, parenthood, children/child-rearing, and divorce?

c). What are your goals and expectations?

d). Are you ready for a commitment in a monogamous relationship?

There are probably as many questions to be asked and answered as there are individuals contemplating marriage. Discussing the answers to the above questions could provide a clue about how prepared you and your potential mate are able to communicate and engage in problem solving.

Couples contemplating marriage may also refer to the following 14 notes as a useful tool for asking the right questions during courtship and while planning for a happy and successful marriage:

1. Commitment

Every marrying couple should be willing to make a lifetime commitment to one another. A psychological and emotional, as well as a physical and financial commitment.

In order to make a marriage last, the husband and wife must be genuinely motivated to make it work. Both must make their marriage a priority. Both must be willing to work towards resolving and removing any and all conflicts that could potentially ruin the marriage.

Although married couples should be committed to one another and their commitment should extend beyond his or her personal goals, it would be an unrealistic expectation to enter marriage with the belief that your spouse will fulfill all of your needs and desires.

It is very important for couples to have a clear understanding of each other's expectation before marriage, to make sure that each is aware of what they are committing themselves to, in the relationship. Unrealistic goals and expectations often lead to disappointment and conflict, which could harm a relationship irrevocably.

Before marriage a man should ask and answer, "Am I mentally prepared to remain faithful and devoted to one woman for the rest of my life?" "Do I expect my wife to take the full weight of making a success of the family as a homemaker, at the expense of her other interest and self-fulfillment needs?" Another vital question, How do you feel about your wife having a higher education, a professional career, and earning a higher salary?

A woman should ask and answer, "Am I emotionally prepared to stand by my man through the thick and the thin?" Do you expect your husband to be the sole "wage earner" or "bread winner," or do you expect him to be an equal partner and share in child-rearing?

In today's society, men and women are much more

educated and are having fewer children. Some are choosing careers over the traditions of marriage and family life. Increasingly, we are witnessing more men being taught how to nurture. Many are opting to stay at home and assist in the rearing of their children while the wives remain employed outside of the home.

Many career women are rejecting the title of "care taker" and are asking, "What about me?" And rightly so, because marriage should not deprive women of their identity. Neither should marriage be a one-sided relationship, with one feeling neglected and sacrificing his or her needs for the sake of pleasing the other. Both, husband and wife, should be able to reap the emotional benefits from the marriage through mutual sharing and caring for one another's needs and desires.

Several case studies show that the second reason for divorce behind a lack of effective communication is due to a lack of money or poor financial planning.

I have known several couples who thought it was unpopular to discuss money matters or individual assets before marriage. Some believed that financial discussions before marriage will create doubts about one's commitment.

On numerous occasions, I have tried to impress upon others the idea that financial planning is necessary before and during the marriage to avoid the primary reason for most divorce conflicts.

Ask yourself these questions, "Do you know your mate's credit score or history, and is that something you think you should know before marriage? Will you keep separate checking and savings accounts or will there be only a joint account? How will financial plans for health care, family planning, vacations, and recreational activities be decided? Who will assume responsibility for financial record keeping, disbursing household bills, and debt management?" Those money matters may sound trite, but are very important and require serious discussions and a satisfactory agreement.

During the process of planning the wedding ceremony, some couples appear more committed towards impressing their friends than making plans for a successful marriage. One particular couple spent over thirty thousand dollars for an elaborate wedding, afterwards they had to move in with the groom's parents until they could pay off the balance of their wedding bills and save enough money to rent an apartment. The emotional conflicts of living with parents and in-laws, in addition to their financial disappointments almost caused the break up of their marriage.

Wise planning before marriage could help clarify your goals and commitments. As well as help reduce potential financial disagreements, which could become a strain on your marital relationships.

Financial planning will also help couples stop living from pay check to pay check and being identified as a the working poor, to a couple with a solid saving account, with the ultimate goals of becoming homeowners and developing sound investments for a financially secure future.

For affluent couples not experiencing money problems, financial planning could serve as a tool to avoid suspicion and remove doubts about one's commitment to the relationship.

There is strong evidence that marital relationships appear to be stronger when couples focus on the spiritual and emotional aspects of their marriage—capable of fostering love, friendship, personal growth, a healthy relationship, and a happy family life. Rather than view their marriage as just another "legal contract" bound by societal laws and rules, or as an "economic institution," just to have someone help pay the bills or take care of you.

A real commitment in marriage is when a husband and a wife faithfully and responsibly honor their pledge to take care of each other emotionally, physically, and financially for the rest of their lives.

2. Effective communication

Communication is an exchange of feelings, thoughts, opinions, and messages—verbally or non-verbally.

Effective communication has long been viewed as one of the key ingredients for unlocking the mystery of romance. In addition to love, sharing, caring, and learning about each other's likes and dislikes. It involves every aspect of a marital relationship and should start before the first date.

In a marriage, effective communication should include the freedom and ability to talk about one's feelings and opinions openly and honestly without verbal or physical abuse—shouting, name-calling, monopolizing the conversation, or constantly bringing up past hurts and wrongs. It should also include the ability to listen attentively without sarcasm, accusations, interruptions, or walking out during the conversation.

Individuals contemplating marriage would be wise to consider learning effective communication skills during courtship and practice the technique until it becomes a natural part of their relationship. It is difficult for a relationship to survive without a pattern of effective communication.

One couple, married for eight years, discovered their inattention and poor communication caused them to feel estranged.

The husband had been reared by his father as an only child. He had been taught that a man should never express his emotions or let others know what he was thinking or feeling. As a young boy, whenever he was upset or feeling distressed, he would participate in sports, lift weighs, or just "hang out with the boys." He developed a pattern of relieving his stress and tension during sport related activities, rather than talking about feelings and emotions.

The wife, was born into a strong two-parent family and was the oldest of five siblings. She had been taught to express her emotions rather than conceal them.

Their marital conflict and lack of communication were producing a lot of stress, which led to a loss of sexual desire, and lack of emotional and physical arousal.

The distance in their relationship was driving them to the brink of separation. The wife initiated individual counseling after her husband refused to consent to joint therapy. Further efforts to engage the husband in counseling also failed. He did not believe in counseling and said, "No one could fix" their marriage other than he and his wife.

The wife continued individual counseling. She described feeling alienated and unappreciated when her husband regularly left her alone "every weekend" without informing her of his whereabouts, or discussing his activities, or friends. She suspected that her husband was unfaithful.

After a few weeks of venting her feelings, frustrations, and discussing various methods of communication. She reported feeling less stressful. She said her efforts to engage her husband in conversation was improving, but expressed her frustration about being left at home, alone, while he goes "out every Friday and Saturday night."

While describing the conflicts in her marriage, she revealed that her husband's most frequent complaint was that she was "too bossy," and her "bitterness" kept him from "feeling like a man" in her presence.

During one of her office visits, she described what she said was her final effort to engage her husband in a serious conversation about the future of their relationship, before she would make an independent decision. She went shopping on a Thursday.

On Friday evening, her husband arrived home as usual, took a shower and started dressing for his regular weekend activities, which remained unknown to her. After her husband took his shower, she took a bubble bath, put on an elegant negligee, expensive perfume, and removed her scarf to show off her new hair style.

Upon leaving the house, her husband stopped at the door.

He asked, "Where are you going?"

She replied, "No where."
He asked, "Who's coming over?"

She said, "No one."

He said, "Well, why are you smelling so good and looking so sexy?"
She said, "For you."

He said, "Why are you looking and smelling sexy for me when I'm getting ready to leave the house?"
She said, "You do plan to return home, don't you?"

The wife gave her husband a "wet kiss with a warm smile" and said, "See ya when you get back." Her husband decided to close the door and remain at home for the evening.

After receiving her husband's undivided attention, she used her recently learned communication skills to engage him in a dialogue. She was able to express her feelings of anger and frustration without using profanity, shouting, blaming, or name-calling. She was also able to actively listen to her husband after asking him to share his feelings, needs, and goals for their marriage.

Recognizing the positive change in his wife's ability to express her emotions without hostility, he was encouraged to share feelings he had never revealed. He decided to join his wife for marriage counseling.

Their conversations led to an agreement that they wanted their marriage to last, not for the sake of economic convenience, or as a constant source of conflict and distrust, but as a mutually satisfying alliance.They also agreed to use their counseling sessions to help establish trust, problem solving techniques, and assess the future of their marriage.

The wife's tactics may appear deceptive and compromising, but she was able to find a way to open up channels of effective communication with her husband. Their participation in conjoint therapy helped rekindle the trust, commitment, and romance in their relationship. And ultimately saved their marriage, which both believed made it stronger.

Over the years, I have become acquainted with numerous principles of effective communication. Yet the most important form of communication in marriage is an open and honest exchange, which reinforces a joint commitment as well as other forms of positive communication. The quality of a couple's interaction, based on how they share their feelings and express their emotions in a realistic and truthful manner will determine the true nature of their love, and the future of their marriage.

3. Trust, Honesty, and Respect

Do you trust your spouse implicitly? Do you view your spouse as an honest individual? You said that you love your spouse, but do you like your spouse? Whether you like your spouse or not is most often based on trust, honesty, and respect.

A positive attitude about marriage is another key ingredient for a happy and successful relationship. One must feel good about their spouse in order to feel good about their marriage.

Most happily married couples report that they are each other's best friend, which usually denotes that they view their spouses as honest individuals whom they trust and respect.

The inability to trust and admire your spouse, most often dictates how couples communicate with one another. It also impinges on the level and intensity of their commitment. When couples lose faith in one another, and are unable to communicate with honesty, the quality and longevity of their marriage is also threaten.

Trust and honesty are necessary tools for establishing and maintaining a pattern of effective communication, and in most cases, will help keep a marriage in tact if both partners are motivated to maintain the relationship. They are also principles that should be practiced in everyday life, because all good relationships are based on mutual trust, mutual honesty, and mutual respect.

Entering a marriage improperly or with deceptive motives will not cement a marriage relationship nor provide the strength required for couples to cope when confronted with adversity. A mutual agreement for marriage should be entered into with confidence, respect and love.

Marriage is a serious relationship that requires a serious commitment. Infidelity, dishonesty, and disrespect is a "no win" situation.

In addition to money matters, jealousy has long been identified as another primary cause of arguments in a marriage.

Frequently, jealous behavior is expressed by individuals who have experienced low self-esteem, rejection, and loss of loved ones. Jealousy is often viewed by most people as a sign of immaturity, based on a lack of trust. Especially when there is a pattern of suspicion that is void of any real or factual evidence.

Some of the clients that I have interviewed who were struggling with unrealistic distrust of their spouses were most often individuals who felt worthless, and thereby believed that they were unworthy of a trusting and loving companion.

Trust is often based on attitudes developed earlier towards others, and whether or not they had experiences that taught them not to trust anyone, including themselves.

Disputes about financial responsibilities, jealousy, and trust often disrupts couple's feelings of intimacy. Their unjustified accusations and criticisms usually cause their spouse to lose respect for them as well as widen the distance in the marriage, which could lead to divorce. Professional counseling should help couples develop effective communication and problem solving skills, which could enable them to develop trust, honesty and respect in their marriage.

4. Always be considerate

Even during disagreements, one should always practice being kind, patient, tactful, and unselfish. As human beings, we are prone to make mistakes. Sometimes in the heat of an argument, one might say or do things that he or she will later regret. A good rule of thumb is to try to never say or do anything that would cause irreparable harm to the marriage, or put your spouse in a position that causes him or her to lose their self-respect.

In relationships where one feels trapped or cornered with no way out that would allow them to maintain dignity, can often make it difficult to restore a sense of harmony or balance in the marriage.

Kindness can often help smooth out the rough edges and pave the way for a clearer direction through turmoil, tension, and misunderstanding.

Ideally, in marriage, one should treat a spouse as one's closest friend and an equal partner.

Building a successful marital relationship also requires hard work, dedication, patience, and having regard for the needs and feelings of your spouse.

5. Use conflict positively
It takes two people to marry, but only one is required to end the relationship.

Seldom, if ever, however, is one person totally responsible for the break up of a marriage.

Different attitudes and behaviors, by its very nature can often lead to conflict in a relationship. If we accept the premise that attitudes are developed from past experiences and other external factors that influenced one's life. Then, every man and woman brings into the marriage their internal and external emotions, motives, desires, and needs. It would also mean that their developed attitudes and behaviors helped made them who they are, and will determine how they respond, or react when they are confronted with a crisis.

Every married couple must learn how to get along with each other, which requires making the necessary adjustments— emotionally, socially, physically, and financially, if they want their marriage to last.

By nature, a husband and wife are separate individuals trying to unite as one, in terms of shared values, goals, and mutual agreements about such issues as family planning, child-rearing, and household responsibilities.

It is a natural tendency for a couple to not agree on

every issue or aspect of their marriage. It is, however essential for them to learn how to adjust to each other's likes and dislikes. They must also consider the needs and concerns of each other. To maintain a happy and successful marriage, both must live up to their responsibilities with a willingness to resolve any and all conflicts, without resentment.

Prior to marriage, each made decisions based on their status as a single and independent person. As a bachelor, a man could impulsively decide how he wanted to spend his free time and paycheck. As a married man, he has to decide carefully whether their budget can afford the little red sports car, boat, motorcycle, and annual membership to the golf country club . He also has to decide whether it is fair to spend most of his free time "out with the boys at the sports club" while his wife remains at home, alone. Likewise, for the married woman.

The ability to communicate effectively with your spouse has been known to be one of the best tools for conflict resolution.

Of course, both must be motivated to resolve the problem(s), and be willing to create an environment that is conducive for the growth of a healthy and happy relationship.

It is not a positive sign of a healthy relationship when one member of the relationship does not feel free to express his or her feelings.

Some couples believe that as long as they suppress their feelings, do not complain, or contradict their spouse, that this will prevent arguments and help their marriage. Experience has proven that this is wrong.

Couples need to know that an exchange of ideas and feelings in a respectful environment can stimulate an open and honest dialogue, which may lead to identifying the real source of conflict, as well as mutual values and concerns.

Expressing one's feelings and opinions are quite different from an individual's need to be right, or always win an argument, or putting selfish needs and interest above the best interest of the marriage.

Disagreements can become an opportunity to learn from your mistakes and the mistakes of others. A married couple should always strive to resolve differences, learn from the situation, and move on with their lives. It is ineffective to dwell on the past or allow past mistakes to dictate the future of a relationship.

If either spouse is struggling with issues of trust, power, anger, or lack of self-control, which consistently create problems in the marriage, the best suggestion would be to seek professional help immediately.

To all the couples who are unable to overlook past mistakes and/or differences, but saving your marriage is your priority, it would also be wise to seek professional assistance. Marriage counseling could help couples learn how to turn conflict and differences into opportunities for self-awareness and developing personal growth.

I can think of numerous stories of conflict, or individuals, couples, and families that entered counseling with a multitude of problems, which resulted in an exploration that brought about creative solutions and strengthen their lives. People who are motivated to seek solutions to their problems, often find them. I also believe creativity can grow out of conflict.

6. Solve problems before bedtime

Life is a constant process of adjustments and readaptation to our changing environment. It is not surprising that human relationships often bare the brunt of these sudden and abrupt changes. One of the options available to human beings is the ability to communicate, which allows us to solve problems and resolve conflicts.

Because all human beings make mistakes, sometime or the other, during their lifetime. The process of forgiving is vital to any and all effective conflict resolutions.

Married couples should be willing to resolve conflicts and forgive one another for past mistakes, even if he or she is reluctant to forget. Especially if the mistake is not part of an established pattern or repeated behavior.

Forgiveness, is an essential part of making-up and moving on in a successful marriage.

Couples need to understand that nothing lasts forever, not even life. Nothing should be left undone or unsaid if it will bring you closer or improve your relationship.

It is common knowledge that no one should go to bed angry. Married couples are no exception. As a matter of fact married couples should make it part of their emotional marital contract to solve marital conflicts before bedtime even if it means staying up all night until you both reach a solution or at least a compromise without feeling compromised.

Studies have shown that the quality of one's sleep is often hampered by anxiety, especially when you are sharing a bed or bedroom with the person you are feeling anxious or emotionally upset with.

Struggling with insomnia or the lack of a good night's sleep will not only impede your objectivity—ability to think clearly and rationally, but affect you health and longevity.

Resolving any and all disputes with your spouse before bedtime is a healthy choice for you and your marriage.

After you have successfully resolved your dispute, if possible, seal your agreement with a handshake, hug, kiss, or good sex. The latter, has been known to induce good sleep.

7. Do not take your spouse for granted

This could lead to feeling unappreciated, frustrated and angry.

Couples who are taking one another for granted are more likely to let their marital relationship become just another routine of sharing a house for economic, social, and legal reasons.

Some where along the way, after a few years of marriage, some couples decide that it is no longer necessary to continue being charming, exciting, entertaining, or maintain a level of humor and fun in their relationship.

After ten or more years of marriage, some relationships start losing favor, or turn sour. I have heard many describe their marriage as boring. Like infidelity, money problems, and lack of effective communication, boredom in a relationship ranks high among the major conflicts leading to divorce. Boredom has led many couples to start taking each other for granted and wonder if they have fallen out of love with one another.

When couples start believing they have fallen out of love, frequently, some of them give up and stop trying to improve the relationship. In some cases, they adopt the belief that they married the wrong person, or wonder if that illusive "one perfect person" is still out there somewhere, who can make them feel whole, complete, or become a better "better half" than the one they married. Such idealistic thinking can lead one to stray— exploring to see if the grass is greener on the other side. Just to discover that the grass on the other side also has to be mowed, watered, fertilized, and nurtured. In most cases, unless they resolve the conflicts in the first relationship, they will repeat the same patterns. Especially, if the cause of the problem is due to unresolved conflicts stemming from childhood.

Two of the most effective ways to avoid taking your

spouse for granted, first, make your marriage a priority above your selfish needs. Secondly, relinquish your need for power and control in the marriage. Never let your marriage develop into an "I'm the boss," soap opera type of relationship.

Ideally, it would be wise to treat your spouse as you desire to be treated.

In an age of dual career couples, women are increasingly rejecting the notion of the husband being labeled "head of household." Women are demanding to be treated as an equal partner in the marriage, even if the husband is the sole wage earner.

Of course, there are still many women who desire to maintain the traditional form of marriage similar to their mother's relationship with their fathers. These women grew up observing their mother recognize their husbands as "head of household" and "sole provider." They proudly described their mother as a "house wife and mother," and as the mainstay of the ties that bound their families together. To them, their mother is a heroine, and someone they would like to emulate. These were the women who described a traditional marriage as one where both husband and wife acknowledged and respected each other's contribution to the relationship without bitterness or feeling victimized.

Following numerous interviews with married couples, it appeared that the most successful and long lasting marriages were the traditional form of marriages where couples lived according to "old fashioned" family and Christian values, based on Bible principles. In those marriages, the wife felt comfortable being identified as a housekeeper, and the husband proudly accepted the identity as the "bread winner." Both felt equally as important in their respective roles, and neither believed that their efforts were taken for granted.

Some of the marriage counseling interviews included women who were employed outside of the home, as well as women identified as house wives. It was revealed that couples who had found an effective way of communicating with one another were more often in tune with each other's intellectual, social, and sexual needs, and were more apt to describe feelings of personal satisfaction in their marriage.

Of course, there are many successfully married dual-career couples. One couple, married for 33 years. Both had successful careers, but made family, friends, and church activities a priority in their lives.

From the onset, they established a pattern in their relationship of sharing virtually every aspect of their marital and parental responsibilities. Roles were secondary in their lives. They ignored the notion that the husband would be identified as the sole provider and strict disciplinarian, and that the wife would assume the role as the sole nurturer for their children.

Prior to their marriage, they planned the date, time, place, and invitations for the wedding together. They also discussed family planning, but nature had its own schedule.

For each of their three children, they took separate maternity and family leave of absence from their employment to provide childcare. Until all of their children graduated from high school they took turns chauffeuring them to various after school and church related activities.

After the youngest child graduated from college, and their home became an "empty nest," they had to adjust to having the house all to themselves. Initially, they felt guilty about the amount of enjoyment they experienced from the freedom and excitement of not having the children in the house. Their new found privacy allowed them to recognize that after 33 years of marriage, they were still happily in love. Both indicated the belief that the success of their relationship was because they appreciated one another and never hesitated to express their appreciation or affection, even in front of their children.

Too frequently, many of us take life for granted. By complaining and bemoaning about what we do not have, rather than appreciate everything we do have, including the spouse you selected as your choice for a lifetime.

A marital relationship grows stronger when couples treat one another special—in a way that reflects love, trust, respect, and devotion.

Always let your spouse know that he/she is appreciated. Make it a daily routine to compliment your spouse for good deeds, special favors, or by simply telling him or her how much your life has been enriched by sharing a part of his/her life. It is always nice to hear someone say, "Thank you."

Another good rule of thumb is to not take anyone or anything for granted.

8. Never embarrass your spouse in front of others.

No one likes to feel disrespected, in private, or in public. Condescending behavior, "put downs" or making disparaging remarks, lead to feelings of embarrassment, anger, and low self-esteem.

Lavishing your spouse with praise and compliments often serves as an aphrodisiac. Showing respect for others is also a sign of good character.

The next time you embarrass, or feel the urge to humiliate your spouse, publicly or privately—ask yourself, "How would I feel, if he or she did that to me?"

9. An apology can be healing

Ask yourself, which would hurt more, to admit when you are wrong, or maintain conflict in your marriage because of a need to be right and prove your spouse wrong.

It does not hurt to admit when you are wrong, as a matter of fact, many studies have proven that by admitting and apologizing when you are wrong contributes significantly to the healing of the relationship rather than cause further injury.

In a marriage, couples should be willing to forgive one another, especially if the nature of the conflict does not involve abuse or a life-threatening situation.

Flexibility in a marriage is also very important. In addition to accepting responsibility for a marital rift by simply saying, "I'm sorry, I was wrong."

The act of apologizing appears to be much easier for people who have a positive sense of identity, who have learned how to accept responsibility for their own behavior, and for couples who have accepted the premise that their marriage takes priority over pride, suspicion, or proving whose right or wrong. It also appears as though these are the couples who have a greater chance for maintaining a successful relationship than those who insist on proving whose at fault, or refuse to forget or forgive.

Apologizing is believed to be the first step towards the process of forgiveness—a vital ingredient for conflict resolution.

An apology can be a very helpful healing tool in any type of relationship with the goal of building a healthy alliance.

10. Plan time together

Couples must plan time to be together, no matter how busy their schedules. Even if they have to turn their wireless telephones into a lovemaking machine. A marriage void of sharing quality time together is at risk of becoming a former relationship.

Highly successful professionals with extremely busy schedules are often employed in jobs that require frequent flying from state to state, and sometimes internationally. For this reason, numerous movie stars, entertainers, athletes, and high level executives have encountered a high rate of divorce.

Long-distance marriages have been known to function and survive, depending on the commitment of the two people involved and how efficient they are in planning quality time together.

There are numerous couples living in the same house together, but also complain about not having sufficient time to share with one another. After working a full day in the office, driving the children to and from their extra-curricular activities, attending parent/teacher's conferences, shopping, doing the laundry, taking the car to the repair shop, and a host of other obligations. Some couples complain about not having enough time in their day to make time for one another.

A 26-year-old career mother of a five and three year old, complained that between her job and children, she is so stressed out at the end of the day that she does not have any energy left for intimacy with her husband.

One man complained that he feels so tired and drained after he arrives home from work, he does not do anything other than drink a beer and watch television until he goes to sleep. The only time he and his wife engage in intimacy is during the weekend, unless she initiates the activity.

The following suggestions are for couples struggling with hectic schedules:

1. Make a list of all the pleasurable activities you and your spouse enjoy together.

2. Coordinate your work and time off schedules with you spouse's schedule.

3. Plan your daily, weekly, monthly, and yearly social activities ahead of time.

4. Make maximum use of telephone conversations, e-mails, and fax correspondence. Writing love letters can serve as a potent reminder of each other's affection, as well as stimulate a desire to share time together.

Couples who are able to see each other daily, but complain about feeling too tired to do anything after work other than lie on the sofa, watch television, and sleep should also plan their daily activities. Including time for a quiet evening together. They should plan time to take short walks together, or go some place where both can relax. Plan time to attend church and/or social events together. Plan for time to invite enthusiastic friends and family members over for dinner or a social gathering.

While sharing time together, couples should separate the time planned for pleasure and relaxation from the time planned for taking care of work related and household obligations. Make a rule, not to discuss business or stressful aspects of your life during your shared quality time for enjoyment. Focus your time and energy on the positive conditions of the life you share together.

A good rule of thumb, is for married couples to maintain a social calendar, which includes time for intimacy as a top priority.

11. Space is important

As one who understands the concept of togetherness. I have also learned to recognize some married couples' need for space. In this day and age when both husband and wife are employed, the demands of their respective employment and other obligations are less likely to allow very much time for unplanned relaxation. Most human beings require some degree of privacy, where they can unwind and think about matters other than work, and daily obligations.

During many of my interviews, I have heard married couples express the need for "space." This required space was often desired away from their employment, spouse, and family members. They described a need to seek solitude for self-discovery without the pressure of meeting marital and/or parental obligations. They expressed the belief that being granted a brief amount of time or "space" without guilt, would allow them the freedom and privacy to improve the quality time with their spouse and children.

In lieu of taking separate vacations, I have often asked couples if developing outside interests and hobbies together would be a better idea. Sharing activities that would allow them the freedom to relax, enjoy themselves, and contribute to a sense of emotional stability.

As an advocate for togetherness–couples sharing activities and as much time together as possible, it is not my intention to dismiss nor exclude the importance of self-discovery. Every human being, married or single, should take regular inventory of his or her life and seek solitude when necessary to recharge their energy for self-revitalization. Especially, if it will enable him or her to become a calmer and better husband, wife, or parent.

12. Maintain good grooming and hygiene
A frequent complaint from many couples after taking their marital vows is that their spouse stop taking care of his/her body. They complain about offensive body odor, bad breath, unkempt appearances, and the fear of their mate losing their health due to neglect or obesity. Most experts agree that how we feel about our bodies is closely link to our self-esteem, and can enhance or interfere with our social life.

Brushing your teeth, taking a daily bath or shower,

using deodorant, putting on clean fresh underwear and outerwear should not be restricted for dating only.

In one situation, a wife refused to kiss her husband because he had several cavities, missing teeth, and bad breath. The husband, absolutely refused to consult a dentist for necessary dental repairs, until his wife gave him an ultimatum.

A person with a healthy mind, body, and a positive disposition is usually recognized as having inner strength and beauty, which is often reflected outward.

Married couples need to know, even if you do not look like Mr. Muscle, or Mrs. Beauty pageant, you can still be well groomed and behave in a manner that will help your spouse find you physically attractive.

Making a conscious effort for grooming, regular exercise, and paying attention to your health care needs will not only help make you attractive and sexually appealing to your spouse, but will contribute to your longevity.

When married couples feel physically attracted to one another, certain brain chemicals known as neurotransmitters send messages through the central nervous system, blood stream, and muscles, from the part of the brain known as the "pleasure center" to the sexual organs of the body, causing sexual stimulation.

These brain chemicals or hormones, appeals to the five senses of sight, smell, taste, touch, and sound. If you accept the premise that the mind or brain is the pleasure center of the body, which stimulates the release of certain chemical substances called hormones. Then perhaps you also understand how these chemical substances, hormones, or neurotransmitters send messages throughout the human body, which can cause an arousal, pleasant feelings, urges, and desires.

Several scientific studies reveal information about the erogenous zones of the human body. Studies show that there are over five million neurological receptors in the body sensitive to sexual stimulation. It has been proven that touching, kissing, and massaging is stimulating and healing for many.

Just as touching, kissing, or just a good body massage can stimulate hormones or sexual drives, which lead to feelings of euphoria, so can one's appearance, smell, language or sound create feelings of excitement. On the other hand, bad breath and body odor have been known to lessen the desire or interfere with the effectiveness of such stimulations.

Generally, after couples have been married for several years, they will become aware of various changes. It is natural for certain physiological changes to occur with aging.

As adult human beings continue to age, hormones, such as testosterone and estrogen, which are responsible for male and female sexual stimulation begin to decrease. When sexual desire starts to diminish, people should consult their medical doctor. Today, amid highly advanced medical technology, there are several remedies available. In addition to various kinds of medications, diet, proper nutrition, regular exercise, and vitamins have also helped raise the level of hormones for increased sexual energy in some healthy men and women.

A few broadcast news' programs and articles written about gerontological research have revealed how some healthy couples who maintain proper hygiene and good grooming habits can find each other attractive, and ways of enjoying each other's company.

I have heard couples describe how patience, kindness, tender loving care, thoughtful acknowledgements, and how letting your spouse know how much you love him or her can also serve as an aphrodisiac to elevate sexual interest, and energy.

So, whether you are planning to marry, newly weds, or have been married for more than 25 years. You should maintain good grooming habits, take care of your health, and try to enjoy life and your marriage.

13. Never let a day go by that you do not express your affection

There is something very magical about the words, "I love you." In addition to observing the interaction of clients in my office during counseling, I have personally learned about the healing qualities of these words. I have also learned that there is a difference between love and affection. Love usually denotes very strong or intense feelings, whereas, affection refers to an expression of those feelings.

Expressing your fond feelings of affection daily will greatly contribute towards maintaining the love in your marriage.

Have you ever heard or read about couples identified as having the "perfect marriage," getting a divorce, after being married for twenty or thirty something years?

There were several couples involved in long-term marriages who said they love one another, but the boredom was causing a distance in their relationship. The gap between their involvement in sexual activity was growing longer and was making it more difficult for either to initiate intimacy or feel romantic.

Frequently, in such cases, the husband complained about his wife not showing any desire for intimacy. The wife complained that she required more stimulation than her husband appeared willing to offer.

After several years of marriage, far too often, many couples focus more on the burdens of their marital responsibilities—paying the bills, childrearing, employment, and household maintenance. In so doing, they spend the better part of their youthful years building their careers, making improvements to their home, and raising their children, but allow their marital relationships to become stale—no passion or excitement. Mostly because they no longer see the need to maintain romance as a high level of priority. Some believe they no longer need to remind their spouse daily of their feelings, or, as many have stated, "my spouse already know how I feel, therefore, he or she doesn't need to be told, I love you."

By regularly letting your spouse know that you still have romantic feelings towards him or her will also help maintain some of the spontaneity or sparks, which ignited the initial flames.

I think, most people will agree, that in addition to trust, honesty, and respect, it is really love and affection, which helps make the glue that leads to longevity and a successful marriage.

Of course, in our modern and sophisticated society, there are many that ask, "What's love got to do with it?" As an "old school" believer, I think love has everything to do with everything in life.

Imagine how special you would feel if your spouse regularly left a love note for you each morning before leaving for work, or waking up and finding a rose on the pillow next to you in bed.

A kind word and an expression of acceptance and appreciation can often make the difference between having a good day or a bad one, feeling good about yourself, or feeling rejected.

Of course, we all know that fulfilling your career and parental responsibilities are important for maintaining a successful family life and relationship, but expressing fond or tender feelings for your spouse will most certainly do more good than harm.

14. Spoil Your Spouse (SYS)

This one is best left to your imagination, based on the knowledge of your spouse's likes and dislikes.

An effort to spoil your spouse is about making that special person who shares your life, happy, while doing something that you know they will enjoy, immensely.

Efforts to spoil your spouse could run the gamut, from planning a vacation to take your spouse to a tropical resort in the Caribbean, Bahamas, Mexico, or Hawaii.

Just think how much you and your spouse would enjoy a romantic get-a-way in the Poconos or a cruise to Cape Cod, Martha's Vineyard, and Nantucket.

For couples with young children, spoiling your spouse could also include making arrangements for the primary caretaker to take a respite, by hiring a baby sitter and sharing a carefree and romantic weekend in a local hotel a few blocks from your home, or to a cabin in the mountains. How about cooking your spouse a special meal served by candlelight, or pouring the water for your spouse to take a warm luxurious bath and offering to scrub your wife or husband's back.

And of course, according to my wife, "There is always the popular shopping spree."

Well, I think you get the picture, but do spoil your spouse in a way that will make your wife or husband feel special and appreciated.

The institution of marriage should be preserved and respected for the protection of the most valuable institution of a democracy—the family.

Chapter V

10 "OLD SCHOOL" NOTES ON PARENTING

One of the attendees at my lecture on parenting, referred to me as "Old School," after my statement about remembering the days when adults used to take the time to chastised their neighbor's children as well as their own. I remember the times, before television and the internet, when parents talked to their children about the "old days." Children enjoyed listening to their parents' stories when their primary entertainment was playing "make believe" games at home with their siblings and talking to one another about their hopes and dreams.

During my employment as a marriage and family counselor in 1971, I was invited to give my first professional public speech in Stamford, Connecticut at the Westover Elementary School's PTA meeting. My message was brief and structured to let the parents know that I was deeply interested in their children's education. A few weeks after my scheduled talk, arrangements were made between the school's principal and the agency where I was employed, for me to visit the school one day per week to conduct counseling sessions with parents and students, including consultation with the student's teachers and speech therapist.

Over the years, my professional counseling experiences, personal life, and role as a parent has taught me much about parenting. I know that the emotional bond between a parent and child can be one of the most rewarding experiences of an individual's life. I also know that when that bond is broken it can be one of the most painful.

Millions of women and men greet parenthood with a tremendous amount of positive excitement and expectations about the joy and satisfaction child-rearing will bring into their lives. Yet there are many that view parenthood as a potential crisis in their lives. They believe that having children will hamper their career opportunities, thwart their social life, or cause conflict in their marriage. Perhaps many of the negative attitudes about parenthood are caused by living in a modern society that often glorify being independent, childless, and self-centered.

Increasingly, it appears that views on traditional family values, roles, lifestyles, and positive expectations are often relegated to conversations about history. Based on the premises that many people view family values as a concept describing family life in the forties and fifties, or as a popular political topic to win votes. Some people view discussions about family values as archaic and inappropriate for the new millennium. Such beliefs have led to a great deal of confusion among many parents about their roles and relationship with their children.

Even sociologists are confronted with numerous questions about the future of motherhood and fatherhood. There are many studies examining the question of whether the need for nurturing and caring for children until they reach adulthood has changed very much from the parenting of the pre-cultural revolutionary years of the sixties and the seventies. Most would agree that the family as an economic unit, where the men hunted and assumed the role as the sole provider and head of household, and the women remained at home, prepared food and tended children are long lost roles and patterns of family life.

With the growing influence of society, politics, the media, and technology, there are several influences affecting the structure of the family as a basic social group. Consequently, the rights of parents and their relationship with children have changed. Seldom do I meet parents who are still teaching their children to unwittingly trust other adults, or insisting that their child say "yes ma'am, yes sir, thank you ma'am/sir, or may I please." If one were to take a survey, it would probably not be a surprise to learn that modern day parents consider such teaching as an old fashioned value that is no longer applicable for today's standards of child-rearing. Of course, many would agree that children reared with such old fashioned values are often the most trustworthy and responsible members of our society. Therefore, one might conclude that it could be considered an effective parenting tool to use some of the parenting methods of the past with some of the modern day techniques for the purpose of raising children to become productive members of our highly technological society.

Bear with me for a few seconds. Just suppose parents in the new millennium could teach their child how to respect themselves and others, how to be more responsible and cooperative, how to be a happier child while engendering skills that will enable them to grow up and develop mutually satisfying relationships. In addition to, how to read, write, count, and use the computer.

Yes, it is well known that most parents in the forties and fifties did not have to contend with the fast paced, highly stressed technological society of the new millennium. They did not have to compete with television, video games, or the internet to raise their children. Nevertheless, some of the parenting skills of the past can be effectively practice today to help children learn how to cope, survive, and develop good character.

In the "old days" parents and some schoolteachers had more control over children. In the forties and fifties, many parents and teachers believed, "If you spare the rod, you spoil the child." However, the growing controversy about child abuse led to laws passed in the 1970s against the use of corporal punishment, which coerced parents and teachers to search for alternative methods of disciplining.

It is still debatable, whether parents in the new millennium, many of whom work two or more jobs, have more leisure time to share with their children than parents of the forties and fifties, who reportedly, worked from "sun up to sun down." However, modern day parents should also be commended for not being afraid to change with the times, and for discarding some of the ineffective methods of the past with new methods of child-rearing.

Today, very few children are growing up having farm work to perform or animals to feed every morning before leaving home for school. Most parents in the new millennium are raising children in urban or suburban areas. Often without the emotional support and protection of extended family members that was once prevalent. Yet many are finding new ways to instill valuable life skills, positive behavior about work ethics, religion, education, family values, and social relationships.

One of the most important roles of parenting is to help children grow up to become self-reliant and productive members of society. I also believe that practicing the following 10 suggestions can contribute towards effective parenting:

1. Nurture a positive sense of self

As part of the human growth and developmental aspects of life, all human beings develop a sense of him or herself based on different perceptions, beliefs, and feelings about who they are, as individuals.

An individual with a positive self image or positive sense of him or herself is often referred to as having self-esteem, which is directly related to one's sense of self worth.

It is important that children learn to evaluate themselves with a positive perspective. How one see oneself most often dictates how one gets along with others, plan their life's goals, make career decisions, and influence how choices are exercised.

All parents should be aware of the fact that while they are sharing their feelings and establishing a bond with their newborn through personal attention, touch, play, and the sound of their voice, they are creating the emotional climate in which the child starts learning who he or she is and what he or she can believe about him or herself. These learning experiences help shape the development of the child's positive or negative attitudes and behavior, as well as build a foundation for a long-lasting bond and trusting relationships.

There are compelling evidence that most people who have difficulty trusting others are mostly people who have experienced a great deal of emotional and/or physical abuse, neglect, and rejection during the most vulnerable stage of their life—from birth through childhood.

I think most people would agree with the premise that trust is something we all build slowly over a period of time based on our interactions with others, starting with our parents or guardians. Of course, as we grow older there are several others with whom we come in contact with on regular basis that also makes an impression on our lives. Such as other family members, playmates, neighbors, and schoolteachers.

Over the years, I have observed the results of some of the people whom I knew during their childhood. Some of them reported growing up feeling loved and wanted by their parents or guardians. Some complained of having only negative memories of their childhood because they were most often made to feel like a nuisance whom nobody loved or cared about, in their home, neighborhood, or school.

The ones who grew up in homes that allowed them the freedom to mature and develop a positive sense of self, appeared to have made the necessary adjustments for establishing productive careers, marriage, family, and good friends.

The ones who grew up feeling unloved and unwanted with low self esteem, seemed unable to believe in themselves. Many were filled with such intense self doubts that they were afraid to try or put forth the slightest effort towards being successful. They described their adult lives as struggling with one employment and/or relationship problem after another.

Today, in the midst of sophisticated technology, resources, and   economic prosperity, I still hear parents complain about a lack of accessible resources which could provide them with better parenting skills.   Many have described how difficult it is to raise a family in a culture where the media, the government, and the internet have a stronger impact on the thinking of their children. To those parents, I urge you to not give up and to continue trying, to the best of your ability, to raise your child in such a manner that will help your child develop a positive sense of self, a secure and emotionally healthy life, so that they can become productive members of society.

Parents should strive to make their children feel loved, accepted, and important. It's an effective method for building trust, confidence, and a positive sense of self. Always compliment your child for their positive conduct and attitudes. Tell them how beautiful and smart they are, and encourage their goal-oriented initiatives.

A child growing up with self confidence is more likely to like him or herself, which would make it more likely that they will learn to trust, respect, and like others.

2. Foster acceptable social behavior

Parents should start teaching their children at an early age that there are consequences for their actions. An effective way to start teaching a child acceptable social behavior in a society of rules and standards of conduct would be to establish and define age appropriate rules, boundaries, and expectations within the home.

Starting from birth, children are regularly exposed to various learning experiences from parents, family members, peers, teachers, and the mass media—all provide different types of positive or negative stimulation, which contributes towards them adopting particular attitudes. It is important that a child's first positive influence starts within his or her home, hopefully, around people who love and care about them.

In many cases, it seems as though, a child who has been taught to obey and respect their parents at home, tend to be more respectful of their teachers and other authority figures outside of the home.

It has been observed, that many children growing up without being taught table manners or how to conduct themselves at dinner time, often find themselves in embarrassing situations when they are in the company of people who expect etiquette or proper social conduct.

Part of positive parenting, should include house rules, and structured activities which allows a child to learn what is expected of him or her. Such rules, could enable children to better structure their time, activities, and relationships with confidence, even in the midst of outside pressure and influence.

Several sociological studies have revealed, children who grows up observing parents and their peers enjoy smoking, drinking, and occasionally using drugs, often form the belief that these self-destructive activities are acceptable social behaviors.

In today's society, too many children appears to be obsessed with watching television, which often expose them to different forms of obscenities, aggression, gender conflicts, and racial stereotypes.

Some of these children are learning that beer commercials with attractive celebrities are recognized as acceptable entertainment, and are often considered one of their favorites.

Without parental supervision, many of these children are unable to differentiate between acceptable social behavior and addiction. Some are having problems separating the violence they watch on television as entertainment from the reality of their violent behavior with playmates.

By watching television without adult supervision, or parental moral persuasion, some children are learning various stereotypes about racial, cultural, and religious groups, which are impacting their relationships with others who appear differently. Consequently, some are adopting the beliefs that it is acceptable behavior to hate and mistreat others.

Again, there are always exceptions to the rule, but in most cases, if a child grows up learning from their immediate environment that it is not proper to lie, steal, cheat, act rude, or do whatever they want to do without regarding the rights of others, they are more likely to conduct themselves accordingly in public.

Teaching children to retaliate with violence is not viewed as acceptable social behavior, and will not prepare a child for a productive future.

Parents should never view their toddler's temper tantrums, kicking or knocking over furniture, hitting, spitting, or biting as "cute" or "child's play." It could be an early sign of developing behavioral problems. Even a toddler should be taught how to respect other children, share their toys, and how to pick up and put away their toys after playtime.

Starting at an early age children should be allowed to play and have fun, while learning how to develop sensitivity to the needs of others. During play time, children learn how to develop relationships, establish trust and gain acceptance. Play time, is also a time most children evaluate their competition skills, personal strengths, and limitations.

Fighting and other ill mannered behavior often leads to an unfavorable reaction from peers and the greater society, which could cause rejection, alienation, and low self-esteem. Several case studies indicate that the seeds of domestic violence starts in childhood with poor impulse or self control.

One of the surest ways parents can prevent or help reduce the frequency of domestic violence is by teaching their sons and daughters how to fulfill their emotional needs, vent stress, and resolve emotional conflicts with acceptable and productive behavior. Starting at an early age, males and females need to learn how to express their feelings with words rather than physical violence. Children who are able to confide in, or talk freely with their parents, guardian, or a responsible and trusting adult are less likely to develop anti-social behavior.

Teaching your child acceptable social behaviors will not only help them learn how to get along with others, it will also help pave the way for a productive future.

3. Encourage problem solving abilities

In addition to making sure a child has a "roof over his or her head, food to eat, and a place to sleep" parents should try to provide their child with sensible guidance, but they should not be expected to solve all of their child's problems.

I know it is very hard for some parents to restrain themselves from becoming too emotionally involved in their child's problems, nevertheless, parents should avoid the natural impulse to solve all of their children's problems, by allowing their child to learn how to solve their own problems by themselves.

A parent should, however, listen to their child's problems, help their child learn how to assess their own situation and use good judgement to the best of their ability.

Parents should use every available opportunity to teach a child how to solve problems and negotiate conflict resolutions. Even a toddler should start learning about how to exercise his or her choice and self-control, as well as how to exercise self-restraint.

Young children love to ask lots of questions, especially precocious four and five-years-old. Of course, I have also known quite a few three-years-old who could ask some shocking questions. No matter how surprise you are with their question, never punish them for asking, or stifle their inquisitiveness.

Asking questions are part of a learning process, and asking the right questions can help solve problems.

Living in a complex world where we are constantly bombarded with numerous commonplace problems, it is imperative for parents to equip their child with the necessary knowledge and skills on how to solve problems and negotiate conflicts.

There are several ways parents can start teaching their child at an early age how to solve problems. One simple example, is when a toddler drops a toy, allow him or her to retrieve it rather than picking it up and giving it back to him or her. After you have shown them how to pick up their toy, just observe how the child will use his or her problem solving ability to retrieve their own toy. A good suggestion is to compliment and enthusiastically praise the child for solving a problem, psychologists call this "positive reinforcement."

If your adolescent son or daughter is emotionally struggling to fit in or be accepted by his or her peer group, take the time out of your busy schedule to listen to their concerns, thoughts, and feelings. Try to understand the child's situation by using what Dr. Thomas Gordon(1918 - 2002), call "the language of acceptance," outlined in his book, "Parent Effectiveness Training (P.E.T.): The Tested New Way to Raise Responsible Children," (1973).

Dr Gordon suggested parents use active listening and language of acceptance without interruptions, lecturing, preaching, moralizing, name-calling, ridiculing, judging, or imposing your view point .

It is far more advantageous to allow your child to find a solution for their own problem, and to feel strengthen by the fact that they have parents willing to listen impartially and objectively.

Teaching children how to set goals and achieve them are also part of learning how to problem solve.

In most cases, the problem must first be identified and defined. One must be able to determine whether the problem is emotional, physical, or mechanical. In either case, problem solving includes asking questions, reasoning or thinking creatively, planning, developing different strategies, and using available resources such as one's intellect, and social or physical ability.

4. Always separate behavior from the child

There is a distinct difference between making a mistake, which is attributable to bad judgement, lack of knowledge, or inattention, and intentionally doing something that you know is wrong.

Young, middle-aged, or old, all human beings make mistakes.

Parents should separate the child's actions or mistakes from the child when disciplining, by letting the child know that they love the child, but dislike the child's negative behavior.

Parents should always let the child know that making a mistake is human, and should help the child understand why what they did was wrong, so that his or her actions will not become a pattern of behavior. It is also important that parents let the child know that a mistake does not and should not define who you are.

Parents should, at all times, use positive reinforcement by rewarding children for acceptable behavior. Most children will seek their parent's approval because they want to feel accepted. In most cases, children are quite willing to please their parents in an effort to gain their approval and acceptance. Parental compliments and praise often goes a long way in motivating a child to improve behavior or strive towards positive behavior to reap more praise and emotional approval.

When parents discipline their children, they are also letting them know that they love them and want the very best for them. Therefore, non-punitive discipline should be humane and geared towards what the American behavioral psychologist B. F. Skinner(1904-1990) called "behavior modification" (encouraging acceptable behavior) rather than just punishment as a means of establishing control or maintaining power.

Instead of hitting a child, there are several other ways a parents can teach a child responsible behavior and the difference between right and wrong. For example, if the replacement cost for a broken window is deducted from a child's weekly allowance after repeated demands not to play touch football, bounce a basketball, or play catch in the house. The replacement cost could be considered punishment by the child, but reinforce the message of responsibility and how important it is to obey household rules.

After completing an instructor training workshop in April, 1976, which authorized me to become an Independent Instructor of Dr. Thomas Gordon's "Parent Effectiveness Training (P.E.T.)," I appeared on WNLK radio talk show in Norwalk, Connecticut to talk about Dr. Gordon's principles of PET, and "Transactional Analysis (TA), a method of psychotherapy" originated by Dr. Eric Berne (1910- 1970).

During the radio program, I attempted to describe how TA and PET could be used to help parents develop more effective ways of disciplining their children rather than use the physical methods of the past. I was surprised when a few callers to the radio station took exception with my views against parents using physical punishment as a means of disciplinary actions.

Amid scientific knowledge and proven theories, there are still many who believed that physical punishment is a parental right, and parent's best method of disciplining. Some parents interpreted laws against using physical punishment to raise children, as laws usurping their parental authority.

During the 70s, in many of my "Parent Effectiveness Training" lectures, I started quoting from published studies about the emotional, physical, and long lasting social effects of child abuse.

Parents were told that when they hit their children as a means of discipline, they are also teaching their child that hitting others is an acceptable way of solving problems.

I believe that children should be allowed to make mistakes, which is part of growing up. I do not believe that physical punishment as a means of discipline is effective. I have read several case studies about children growing up in households where physical punishment were regularly used compared to children who never received physical punishment have shown that children raised with an equal amount of non-punitive discipline and love, most often grow up to become responsible, respectful, resourceful adults, and nurturing parents.

Parents should be encouraged to find effective ways of correcting their child's behavior without the child feeling unwanted, unloved, or flawed for making a mistake.

5. Cultivate positive work ethics

Unless your child is due to inherit wealth, which would allow him or her to live comfortably for the rest of their lives, they need to start learning how to develop positive work habits at an early age.

Even children being raised with maids and nannies should have some type of work related responsibilities or household chores to perform on daily basis, if for no other reason than to help them learn to care about their home environment and surroundings. Sharing in the responsibilities for the upkeep of one's bedroom, home, and community could lead to positive work habits, discipline, and responsible behavior.

In the "old days," parents used to say, "Keep a child busy and you keep'em outta trouble" or "An idle mind is the devil's workshop."

Taking out the garbage, washing dishes, assisting with the laundry, keeping their rooms clean, sweeping down the driveway, raking leaves, or mowing the lawn are some of the chores most adolescents should be able to perform successfully. Household chores should not be considered a form of child abuse when properly structured and supervised.

For many families, assigning children household tasks is one way of introducing a child to the world of work, which helps ease the transition from home and school to starting a career.

Most children are exposed to occupational roles through observing the work habits of their parents, or people whom they meet, or occupations portrayed in the media.

While conducting a seminar on "Conflict Negotiations Between Management and Employees," I was asked to "define Work ethics as it relates to living in a society where people must work to live.?" To paraphrase my response, I said, "Work ethics refers to the values, morals, or attitudes of employees towards their employment, and the rules and regulations which management uphold to protect the rights and freedom of employees within the company or organization." Something to that effect. Today, I would say, work ethics refers to positive work habits which promotes the general health and welfare of society.

The very nature of human life, equips us with certain needs, motives, education, and skills, which assist us in deciding on a career path or goals. Our personality will determine if we are willing to follow established rules, or whether we will achieve our career goals, or if our decisions will lead to job satisfaction or a desired economic status.

Even children whom are born into wealth and are being trained to become owners of industries or corporate executives must learn how to establish and follow rules and regulations that will benefit its employees, business, and society.

Regardless of one's economic status, parents should teach their child that productive employment which promotes the general health and welfare of society, offers various psychological rewards in addition to income, and hopes for financial security.

6.   Help children pursue their personal interest and goals

In addition to performing regular chores at home, children should be encouraged to pursue their personal interests in extracurricular activities at school and/or at church, which often leads to developing initiative, group social skills, team spirit, and leadership abilities. This suggestion is not meant to encourage parents to pressure their children into activities geared towards making them olympic contestants or high powered executives. Extracurricular activities should help students to develop and focus their talents, skills, and special interests in a constructive manner.

Participating in after-school activities should not be coerced, overwhelming, or unduly stressful.

Children should not be rushed into adulthood. Unwittingly, some parents use their children as tools to achieve their own lost or unfulfilled dreams. While forcing their children to deny their youthful energy and instincts to play and have fun. Too many parents pressure their children to succeed with adult expectations.

I have observed children as young as six, seven, and eight years old with overwhelming after-school schedules. Their parents had them enrolled in several activities, which led to some of the children describing anxieties that are usually identified by adults who feel trapped in a fast paced "Rat-race" society.

Of course, some parents are locked into this so-called "Rat-race," by working two or three jobs, with the belief that they need to indulge their child with many of the luxuries of life, and having their child participate in numerous activities represent their success as a parent. Parents should be informed that most children would prefer to spend quality nurturing time with their parents and more time playing and having spontaneous fun with their peers.

After-school or church related activities should be rewarding experiences that lead to healthy habits, meaningful relationships, and positive memories of one's childhood.

Most of us are aware of numerous childhood stars or celebrities who were very successful as children, but felt rejected as adults. The tabloids occasionally writes a report about their whereabouts, revealing how many of them spent the majority of their adult lives unhappy while living with resentment about their inability to succeed as adults.

If we are fortunate enough to live a long life, or until we are considered old, we will spend the majority of our lives during adulthood, which makes childhood a relatively brief stage of life. During our old age, we should be able to reflect on a happy childhood, and take comfort in the fact that we were able to pursue our personal interest and achieve goals.

7. Teach children about financial responsibilities

We are living in an age where materialism appears to represent a certain status of success. Increasingly, many children are refusing to wear anything other than designer clothing. They are demanding that their parents buy them "everything" (materialistically speaking). Some parents believe that buying their children "everything" serves as a substitute for their lack of attention, understanding, and inability to share more quality time.

Even if parents are wealthy they should not contribute to their children becoming materialistic. Parents should be encouraged to help their children strive for self-reliance by focusing on their academic, psychological, social, and physical development.

I have heard and read many stories about people born into impoverished conditions, with parents who could only buy the bear necessities of life. Yet many of these children overcame poverty and became successful. Simultaneously, there are numerous stories about children who grew up with parents that bought them "everything" and became failures as adults because they never learned how to earn their way in society.

One woman echoed a complaint, which I heard from several parents, about their children's obsession with fashions and choice of clothing. She purchased a ticket for her 17 year old son to attend a popular concert. Before leaving the house for the concert she observed her son with well over 2,500 dollars worth of wearing apparel. From his pierced ear rings, gold chains, designer clothing—baggy shirt and pants, down to his top name brand socks and sneakers. When asked where does her son get the money to buy such expensive clothing. She said, "His father buys him whatever he wants." Then she said, "But you know, if I did not know my son and saw him walking down the street, I would probably get off the sidewalk, because he looks and dress like a street thug."

Ten years later, he was still living at home with his mother. The complaint now was that he does not have any ambitions or career goals. At the age of 27 he is still "hanging out" with his friends and "partying."

All parents should teach their child about financial matters. Even if you have very little money or income you can still teach your child the importance of financial planning, savings, and investment. When you go grocery shopping, take your child with you, show them how to become a wise consumer by shopping for the highest quality for the lowest prices. If you are living on a tight budget, let your child assist you in scanning the newspapers' advertisements for discounts and coupons. Help them learn about the importance of comparison shopping at different stores. Show them how to read labels to learn about proper nutrition and product quality .

If you have to save money to purchase a big ticket item, explain to your child the planning involved. Help them to understand that the advertised price does not include the cost for taxes, and/or shipping and handling. If you have to place an item on lay-a-way plan, let them see what's involved.

If you can afford to give your child an allowance, discuss with him or her how much should be received based on your income and other financial responsibilities. Allow your child an opportunity to earn more allowance by performing extra chores around the house. Insist on a portion of their earnings being placed into a savings account or an investment portfolio.

Encourage your child to invest wisely in their future by using a part of their allowance or income to purchase stocks and bonds rather than just on social life spending and designer clothing.

Whether you are a family living on a budget or a family with established financial resources, all children need to learn about money management.

Teaching your child about financial matters is a valuable learning experience, which will undoubtedly make them more productive in adulthood.

8. Promote the importance of education

Since the home is recognized as a child's first learning environment, parents should continue their child's education outside of the home, by becoming actively involved in their child's education at school.

Several studies have shown, when parents are actively involved in their children's education, and their child's school, more often than not, these children are more motivated to succeed and achieve their potentials and life goals.

Outside of one's family, schools have assumed the major role of socialization. In addition to imparting knowledge and skills, schools introduce children to attitudes, morals, and values of the American culture and diversity. For many, schools are an institution where they learned how to assess their intellectual, physical, and social capabilities.

It has often been said, "Education is the key to success."

Parents should encouraged their children to become interested in education and learning. During early childhood everything is considered a new learning experience. Children are curious about their new environment and are eager to learn new information. One way to encourage children's interest in learning is for parents to start reading to their child at a very young age. Parents can start teaching their newborn that learning is fun by reading to them, pointing out different colors, making different sounds, noises, letting them feel the wind blowing, and experience many of the other interesting aspects of their environment.

I have often encouraged parents to read everything that is accessible around their house to their young children. To read books, newspapers, ingredients, labels, cooking instructions, directions, information on packaging materials, as well as how-to-assemble instructions.

In most cases, children who have acquired an early interest in reading are often eager to attend school, and are often the most enthusiastic students.

One of the highlights of my professional career, was having an opportunity to read and talk to a group of first graders at E.L. Bing Elementary School in Tampa, Florida on my 58 birthday . Mrs. Clydeana Weatherspoon Willis had invited me to talk to her class during the "Great American Teach-In" The fact that it appeared on my birthday made it quite a rewarding experience for me. The children greeted me warmly. They were extremely attentive and responsive to questions about the books I read. After reading the first book, the children's enthusiastic response made it obvious that they enjoyed the subject matter and were anxious to show their comprehension.

I was amazed at the rapport Mrs. Willis had established with her students. In many ways she seemed more like a mother with her children than their teacher, but I guess that is what good teaching is all about. As a teacher, Mrs. Willis renewed my belief in our education system, and her students elevated my faith in our future generation.

9.   Advocate sexual morality

Since schools are viewed as an extension of the home and family, parents should encourage the educational system to establish a life learning skills program that would help teach children practical skills that could be applied to age-appropriate daily living experiences, in addition to the basic academic routine. Parents should also be encouraged to teach their children about matters pertaining to sex.

The barrage of "X-rated" sex symbols and messages displayed on the internet, television, movie theaters, and many rap songs are exposing children to negative images of love and sex.

There are still too many children growing up listening to backyard conversations with their peers about "doing it," or "hitting it," and using slang to describe the male and female genitalia, which is often their only source of sex education. Such unsupervised education is increasingly leading towards a growing disrespect of the opposite sex. In addition to the increasing confusion about developing one's sexual identity, behavior, morals, values, and the institution of marriage.

In the past, conversations about sex and articles written on the subject of sex were considered taboo, and/or met with public disdain. Sex education has long been viewed as a private family matter, and accepted as the responsibility of parents, who were expected to teach their children about sex and sexual mores. However, beyond saying "don't do it," some parents feel inhibited about discussing the physiology of human reproduction, functions of male/female sex organs, and the various sexually transmitted diseases. In addition to the fact that many parents feel ill equipped to discuss the social, psychological, and emotional causes and consequences of sexual activity.

Both boys and girls need to be properly educated about the growth and development of human beings. They should be taught age appropriate principles about physiological, psychological, and behavioral differences as their bodies continue growing. Society in general, need to stop describing certain body parts as acceptable to talk about and others as private, embarrassing, shameful, and taboo.

As a social worker, I interviewed many parents that refused to discuss the topic of sex with their children "until they are mature enough to have sex." Consequently, far too many parents reported that their first conversation with their child about sex did not occur until after discovering that their daughter or son had already engaged in sexual activity, was becoming a parent, or had contracted a sexually transmitted disease, which required medical attention.

In 1973, I assisted an outreach worker from Planned Parenthood in conducting a sex education workshop for a group of teenagers. The outreach worker showed a film about various risks that could result from sexual activity. It was an age appropriate and relatively harmless informational film about the importance of sexual abstinence and birth control.

After reviewing the film, a sixteen year old male group participant shyly raised his hand and asked, "What's a vagina?"

A few of the other teenage participants laughed, but when asked to answer the young boy's question, it was surprising to learn that only an eighteen year old female could properly answer the question.

I think most people would agree that engaging in sexual activity require emotional maturity and should be reserved for marriage. However, If we consider the increasing number of teenage pregnancies and sexually transmitted diseases, it should be obvious that many young people are not waiting until marriage before engaging in sexual activities. It is also quite obvious that many young people are not talking to their parents about sex.

Perhaps, if children were properly educated about sex and sexual matters, they might develop a clearer understanding of anatomy and physiology, improve their vocabulary, and become equipped with sufficient knowledge that could enable them to talk more freely to their parents, as well as make rational decisions about their bodies, and their lives.

Parents should be encouraged to talk to their children about sex prior to puberty, and share information that reflects their moral and religious values about sexuality.

Information is empowering and could help protect your children.

10. Parents should serve as role models

As role models, parents should be very careful about the messages they send to their children—intentionally or unintentionally.

A young man was receiving counseling as one of the stipulations for his parole. He had been arrested several times for car theft and other violations of larceny. When asked why he felt the need to continue engaging in criminal activities, rather than seek employment so he could stay out of jail and purchase the things he wanted? The young man described stealing as, "Just another way of life." He reported that he started "petty theft" at the age of six and that he had been exposed to stealing by various family members, including his parents.

The young man recalled going to the grocery store with one of his parents. He observed his parent giving the cashier a $20.00 bill for $12.00 of groceries. The cashier mistakenly gave the parent $18.00 instead of eight dollars.

Outside the grocery store, he listened to his parent exclaimed how much the extra money was needed, without any intention of returning the money.

He also described a resident of his community who was an employee of the cable company, offering free cable service to neighbors for a hook-up fee of $50.00. His family received free cable service without reservation.

Without realizing. it, some parents are also teaching their children how to lie, cheat, and steal.

Some parents are also teaching children how to procrastinate. When children observe their parents consistently putting important things off that requires their immediate attention. "I'll do it tomorrow, I'm tired right now." Some children will adopt that philosophy and feel justified in not completing their school homework assignments, or make excuses for not completing other necessary tasks.

A 14 year old girl in counseling for behavioral problems, recalled answering the telephone and was instructed by a parent to tell the caller that the parent was not at
home. Even though the parent was standing next to her.
The same child overheard a parent compliment another
adult. Shortly afterwards, she heard the parent describe
that person with derogatory comments. She said it was
confusing as to why her parent would punish her for
telling a lie when the parent "lie all the time."

Depending on the child's age, some children do not
have any concept of a "small lie" or a "polite lie." After
being reprimanded for telling a falsehood, most children
learn to recognize an untrue statement as a lie.

Early in life, children start learning about patterns of
communication, relationships, and about how to conduct
themselves around their peers, by observing their parents
and/or guardians. The way a mother and father relates to
one another often serves as a direct message to their
sons and daughters about male/female relationships.

I have met many parents who were quite successful
in serving as role models for their children. Most of them
had effectively taught their children the difference
between right and wrong, acceptable and unacceptable
behavior, and how not to conform with those who choose
to indulge in negative behavior. These were the parents
who started teaching their children at an early age how to
conduct themselves at home before they entered grade
school.

Parents realize that children are the most valuable
resources, in terms of their longevity, genealogy, and for
the future of our civilization.

Not everyone can become president of the United
States of America, chief executive officer of a large financial institution, or play basketball with the finesse, and skill
of a Michael Jordan, but every child can be loved, and

every child should grow up knowing that he/she has value, despite his or her chosen career path.

As parents, we have an obligation to our children, and part of that obligation is the real essence of family values—to help children develop moral judgement, learn the difference between acceptable and unacceptable behavior, how to respect the rights of others, and how to govern their own actions in terms of the established laws of society.

When children are reared to honor, obey, and respect their parents, they also learn to respect themselves and others. They are also more likely to honor their parents by taking care of them when they become older and unable to take care of themselves. Putting family members first is an "old school" idea that is still applicable in today's society.

Without a trace of doubt, I strongly believe, of all the careers and professions of the world, none are more important or carry a heavier responsibility than the role of a parent.

It has often been said, and is widely believed, that the quality of human relationships, life, and survival of the human race, is dependent on human beings' ability to love one another. If this premise is true, who, better than a parent, can start teaching a child about unconditional love, which can transcend into love of oneself, parents, family, community, and love for all the inhabitants of the earth.

Chapter VI

NOTES ON
THE JOY OF FATHERHOOD

The word "Fatherhood" is frequently used to denote the relationship between a man and his offspring, whether it is biological or adopted. Millions of men welcome the challenges of fatherhood and view their individual status as a father as their most significant identity as a man.

As a Certified Independent Instructor of Dr. Thomas Gordon's Parent Effectiveness Training program, I was strongly motivated in my efforts to teach both men and women how to become effective parents.

I was aware of the fact that most parenting classes were attended by mothers, with the conspicuous absence of the fathers. A father is a parent who must also be trained. So, I started including information in my brochures that would encourage fathers as well as mothers to attend my workshops.

During many of my travels and lectures on the importance of fatherhood, as well as motherhood, I have encountered those who concur with my beliefs about the values of positive family ties, but questioned the role of fathers.

I heard many stories about people growing up without their fathers. There were stories about fathers who lived in the home, but were viewed as "absent fathers." Often these fathers worked long hours and spent most of their time outside of the home. They had to get up early in the morning while their children were still asleep, and usually did not return until late in the evening after their children's bedtime. There were fathers described as the "strong silent type" who seldom, if ever, talked or interacted with their children or other family members. They were the fathers that everyone in the family complained about not attending any of the family's church, school, or social activities.

There were also the stories about the fathers who abandoned their responsibilities—especially the ones that became alcoholics or drug addicts in an attempt to escape the painful reality of their frustrations and disappointments.

Over the years, we have been inundated with movies, books, and various articles in magazines and newspapers about the perpetually unemployed fathers who gave up and dropt-out of society, believing that society's unfair demands and expectations were exacting heavy burdens, which prevented them from creating a livelihood and taking care of their families.

Then there are the stories about men known as "playboys," or "sugar daddies"), depicted as the type of men who bragged about having sired many children by several different women, and not take responsibility for any of the children he claimed. Attempts to classify most men in a negative way has often been used to revile the institution of fatherhood.

Then there were the stories about men who denied being the father of their child/children. Such stories became popular during the 90's on television programs featuring guests who appeared on national television shows to talk about their controversial and dysfunctional relationships in front of a live studio audience. It appeared as though, for the sake of ratings, the talk show's host, joined by an excited audience, encouraged the guests to display obnoxious and shocking behavior.

One show, featured women bringing suspected fathers of their children on national television to take a DNA paternity test.

One of the women was adamant in her claim that the man whom she had engaged in a one-night rendezvous was the father of her one-year old son. The man accepted her invitation to appear on the show and admitted he had a one-night affair with her, but was just as tenacious in his disbelief about being the father. He accused the mother of the child as being a "loose woman with loose morals." The woman, in turn, called him "a no good man and a do nothing father."

As members of the audience were laughing at the man and woman's exchange of accusations. Television cameras continued to roll, showing the man and woman emotionally engaged in shouting, name-calling, finger-pointing, and bleeped profanities. Towards the end of the television show, the host revealed the results of the DNA test, which proved that the man was the child's biological father.

Since I have only watched those types of talk television programs once or twice, I am unable to make a value judgement about them, but I have heard several conversations about them from a few coworkers and clients. Recognizing that such shows were viewed primarily as entertainment, I wondered how effective the show that I watched might have been if they had addressed certain questions like, What happens next? To what extent would the father become involved in the child's life? Would there be professional counseling available to help the couple repair their relationship so that joint decisions could be made for the care of the child?

Much has been written and said about the negative images of fatherhood. In order for men to rid themselves of the negative stereotypes about fatherhood, all men must learn how to become effective parents.

Just as there are stories about men who refuse to be responsible for their children, there are millions of untold stories about responsible fathers. There are also thousands of reported cases about mothers who prefer to raise their children alone, without any involvement from the child's father. A large number of these cases involved men who did not know they were fathers until the child became an adult and searched for their biological fathers. There are also situations involving women who feel antagonistic towards their child's father. Some of these women established legal and/or other means to prevent the father's involvement in the life of his child/children.

There are several reported cases about the breakup of good father-child relationships following a bitter divorce between the father and the mother of the child. Consequently, many men have been and are being denied their parental rights to serve as fathers. Frequently, such conflictual relationships results in a cyclical pattern of many children growing up without fathers. Leading to the question of how does a boy growing up without his father learn how to become a father beyond the act of procreating.

Despite the numerous odds against the institution of fatherhood there continues to be millions of fathers actively involved in their children's lives. And there are still a large number of men who continue to view their role as fathers as insignificant and unappreciated. These men, need to know that a large number of women also feel their value and quality as mothers are not always realized. Some women believe motherhood is often taken for granted, nevertheless, most continue their maternal responsibilities, as should the fathers who are allowed to do so.

Men need to learn what most mothers have known since the beginning of life—having a child is a blessing and a responsibility, which some view as a burden. The blessings, however, almost always outweigh the burdens.

Children provide men with a reason for living, as well as serve as an extension of their life, which lets the world know that they once existed. Having a child can also change a man's perspective of life, by giving his life new meaning and a sense of hope for the future.

I have heard many men say that being a father provided them with an opportunity to care for someone else outside of themselves and raising their child was the greatest joy of their lives.

Much of my research during the 1960's, 70's and early 80's about the roles, patterns and functions of the family as a social group led to readily available information on the subject of parenting, motherhood and the dynamics of family life, but scant information about the importance of fatherhood.

Increasingly, in the 90s and the start of the new millennium, more information about the role of fathers were and are being documented and published. Much of the information agree that all children benefits significantly from two involved parents. Most experts, also agree that children's early positive relationships and emotional bonding with their fathers are essential for development of positive attitudes and behavior. It is widely believed, that when fathers are nurturing, children have a better chance of developing higher self-esteem, a sharper sense of perception, and problem solving skills. I have reviewed several cases, as well as known many children who were emotionally attached to their fathers. In most cases, these children exhibited less anxiety about socializing or confronting new situations. They were less likely to use drugs, join a gang, or get involved in criminal activities. They were far more likely to stay in school, graduate, and seek gainful employment.

As much as we read in the mass media about men who neglects their responsibilities as fathers, seldom do we hear or read about the extraordinary fathers who may not be perfect, but make their children a priority in their lives, or about the fathers who attend parent education classes to learn how to become better fathers. Neither do we read or hear much about men who are childless, but desperately wants to become fathers.

When I conduct workshops scheduled for more than one (hourly) session, I try to encourage participants to identify themselves and their needs, by sharing their reason for attending and what they expect to gain from the workshop. This process often allow participates who had never spoken out in a public forum or around strangers to develop their self-confidence in a supportive environment and establish rapport with other participants who can relate to their needs by identifying similar parental problems and issues.

One parent training workshop had 31 participants, which included seven men and 24 women. One of the mothers identified herself as a single parent, raising five boys. She, expressed her gratitude for the seven men in attendance by acknowledging the importance of their input as fathers in addition to the male workshop leader and that she was looking forward to learn something from the male perspective with great anticipation.

One of the men identified himself as a husband and a father of four— one son and three daughters. He decided to attend the workshops so he could learn how to be a father. He grew up without a father or the presence of any positive father figures. He described his relationship with his children as virtually non-existent beyond being a provider. He spends most of his time working. When he has time to share with his children he feels like a stranger. He loved his children. They were the reason why he worked so hard to provide for them, but he did not know how to relate to them on an emotional or social level.

Another male participant, identified himself as an unemployed divorced father of two children, ages four and two, whom he cared for five days a week between seven in the morning and five o'clock in the evening.

He described his daily routine—walking approximately one mile from his rented room to his ex-wife's apartment, preparing breakfast for his children before escorting his four-year-old daughter to pre-kindergarten while pushing his two-year-old son in a stroller. Without the use of a car or transportation, he had to walk seven inner-city blocks each day to and from the school. A task which forced him to realize the importance of fatherhood. Due to their financial situation, which was part of the reason for their divorce, his ex-wife chose to continue her career. Because of the love they shared for their children, they were able to mutually agree on terms for on-going childcare.

His feelings of attachment for his children forced him to actively search for gainful employment. His repeated failures and anxious efforts to become a positive role model led him to hire himself out as a handyman for household repairs on evenings and weekends. He was determined to become a better father and hoped the workshop would equip him with tools for understanding the needs of his children and building a lasting relationship.

A third male participant described himself as a husband and father of three children. He grew up in a strong close-knit two-parent family. He described his relationship with his father as extremely tight. "In addition to being my Dad, he was my best friend." He recalled how his father encouraged him to become interested in sports and attended all of his sporting events. While in high school he was a star athlete, which earned him a full scholarship to play football in college. He was a starting linebacker in his senior year of college when his father died of a heart attack. He described parenthood as hard work, but the best job he ever had. He decided to attend the workshop because of the memories of his Dad and his own desire to be a positive role model for his children.

Throughout my career, I have encouraged childless couples who wanted to become parents, to adopt. Nevertheless, I have listened to several male clients express frustrations about their yearning to become biological fathers. In some cases, these were the same men serving as step-fathers or an adoptive parent. In each situation, each man had his own unique reason for longing to beget a child of his own and pass along his bloodline. Simultaneously, each man had a different reason for his sterility or his wife's infertility.

One man, whom I will call "Hawk," desperately wanted to become a father. Since early childhood, Hawk had dreamed of becoming a father and having a loving family similar to the one he grew up in.

Hawk was an only child, born when his father was 51 and his mother was 40-years-old. Hawk's parents made him feel like he was a special gift from God and their greatest blessing. His parent's years of wisdom caused them to avoid spoiling him with materialism, but lavished him with love, praise, rules, boundaries, and a guided sense of moral purpose.

As much as he desired to have a large family of his own, he decided to plan his life thoughtfully and carefully. His plans included going to college, develop a marketable skill, locate a job with a comfortable income, which would make him a good provider, and search for a wife who would be the love of his life.

At the age of 37, Hawk married a 29-year-old woman named Alice. They spent the next seven years trying, unsuccessfully, to become pregnant.

At the age of 44 and 36, respectively, Hawk and Alice felt compelled to seek medical assistance, although both were healthy and neither had ever had any serious illnesses. Consultation with a physician indicated that there could be several reasons for infertility. Hawk received a complete medical check-up and was tested to determine if he had a low sperm count. Alice was scheduled for tests to determine if she had a blockage in her fallopian tube, endometriosis, or a problem with her uterus. None of their medical examinations revealed a cause for infertility. It was suggested that they have sexual intercourse in a certain position and reduce the frequency of their sexual activities until Alice's fertile cycle to see if that would enhance their reproductive cells.

After two more years of exhaustive medical tests and false positives, Hawk and Alice believed they would not be able to conceive naturally, but ruled out the possibility of trying to conceive through artificial insemination. Despite their disappointment, Hawk remained committed to his wife whom he loved and continued to treat as though she was his greatest gift.

Two years later, after they had given up on having a child and was trying to accept their status as a childless couple, Alice's routine medical check up revealed that she was pregnant, with twins.

At the age of 48 and 40 respectively, Hawk and Alice gave birth to a healthy son and daughter. By all accounts, Hawk was the perfect husband and father. He was known as a nurturing positive role model. There were no doubts about Hawk believing he was the luckiest husband and father alive. His wife and children were described as the joy of his life. Yet he was attending the parenting workshop for positive reinforcement.

It has often been said, "The days of chivalry is long gone." Nevertheless, I still believe that a man can be a gentleman with his girl friend, wife, and/or the mother of his child, without acting like a chauvinist.

Men who maintain chauvinistic ideas and beliefs about their manhood or their roles as fathers, need to change their attitudes and become more flexible towards their wives or girl friends, as well as become more nurturing with their children.

To a large extent, the perceived gap between men and women, and men and their children, can be viewed from a cultural and historical perspective. A pattern of behavior was started back in the days when men were expected to serve solely as protectors and providers, and women assumed the role of caretakers.

According to many anthropologists, the human family has evolved since the beginning of mankind. Historically, a family unit is believed to have consisted of a mother and her offspring. As various individuals became more territorial and hierarchical, men were accepted as part of the group and families were formed as a means of protection. The role of men and women were clearly defined. The men recognized as fathers served as hunters and protectors. Women cooked and tended to the children. The family became an economic and social unit. During those days of history, most men did not require any type of formal education to become a good provider.

Although the role of fathers as good providers and protectors served as important functions within the family unit during those earlier years. The technological and cultural changes made over the years have also changed the nature of men's relationships with their wives and children.

There was a time, in history, when men were barred from attending the birthing of their offsprings, unless they were medical doctors. Some had to wait outside the house until after their child was delivered. Yet, during the same time period, there were several stories told about the gentle and nurturing behavior of farmers who proudly described how they helped a horse or cow deliver a calf, or their dog deliver puppies.

Many fathers talked about growing up as young boys being told they were not supposed to cry or show their emotions. Most were led to believe that the image of a "real man" was one who lived as though he was insulated from, or impervious to pain and emotional feelings. They grew up with images instilled in them of boys being rough and tough, playing with guns, trains, sports, and hunting. During the 40's, 50's, and early 60's many boys received a rifle for their 12th birthday as a symbol of manhood. Much of which were popularized by the famous western movies of this era. While healthy images of girls involved playing with dolls, acting maternal— being attentive to feeding, nursing, grooming, and expressing their emotional feelings.

Of course, many young boys were also led to believe that it was okay, masculine, and much more socially acceptable to play with and take care of (nurture) their pet animals who also had to be fed, groomed, and taken to the veterinarian.

Despite the cultural changes made in our society, and the fact that millions of men are working hard everyday as caring and loving fathers, there are still a few men and women who think nurturing is a feminine trait, especially when it involves father/daughter relationships.

Based on some of the "fatherhood workshops," I have conducted, which include information on the subject of father/daughter relationships, many of these men had never heard or read about the importance of a positive nurturing father/daughter relationship. In addition to the fact, some had never experienced a positive father/son relationship either.

Several studies show that a father's relationship with his daughter is equally as important as his relationship with his son.

Today, it still seems much easier for some men to talk about going hunting, fishing, cars, sports, and/or women in the conquering sense than talks about a positive relationship with their wives and children.

Depending on one's culture and living environment, it also appeared as though some men were discouraged from talking about having a positive relationship with their wives. During the old days, men who were obliged to their wives as loyal and faithful husbands were frequently called "Henpecked." A derogatory term attributed to men believed to be dominated by their wives. In some circles, it was not that unusual for men with low self-esteem to behave in a loving and affectionate manner at home with their wives and act another way in public, especially around other men. One commentary was, at home he was a "Yes dear, man" and around the boys, he would either try to impress upon them that at home he was the "Boss," "Head of his home," and the type of man who "kept his wife and child in check," or avoid talking about his wife and family.

Based on my personal and professional experience, I am convinced that how a father respond to his child's mother is an essential factor in children's social-sexual development, in terms of acquiring healthy attitudes about male/female roles, relationships, and establishing their sexual identities.

Men needs to know that in our modern day society, children are empowered when they see their parents getting along, especially when they act as though they love and care about one another. Living in an environment with unconditional love, where family members are not afraid to express their affections can contribute greatly towards a child growing up feeling safe, secure, and with a strong sense of self confidence.

Today, more than ever, I strongly believe that men who strive to become good husbands, are more likely to be better fathers and positive role models.

During the days of rugged individualism, a man gained recognition and public acceptance based on his status as the sole wage earner. His reputation was often measured by his income or his ability to provide for his family. If he was viewed as a "good provider," he was more likely to be selected as a role model and leader within the community, despite his lack of education or training in any specific skill.

Today, in our fast-paced, always changing society, with increasing technology, most uneducated and unskilled workers have been replaced by sophisticated machinery and computers. In addition to corporate takeovers, mergers, and downsizing, the idea of job security no longer exists.

In this modern era of uncertainty, frequent job changes, and high unemployment within certain communities, some fathers can no longer claim the title of "good providers."

For many men, a child provides the only opportunity for them to serve as a role model in their life span. So, whether a man is the biological father or a father figure in a child's life, all men should know that there is a great deal of joy and rewards in fatherhood.

When a man enters a marital relationship with a woman who already has a child or children, he is, in fact, accepting equal responsibility for the child/children and it should not matter whether he is the biological father or adoptive parent.

All men should be encouraged to view their family as an asset, rather than as a liability. Men should know that fatherhood extend beyond just a financial responsibility. Even if you are unemployed or underemployed, a child still needs a father's love, time, and guidance.

Now, what about the positive? Surely, there must be numerous positive revelations about the institution of fatherhood.

For a father to help nurture a child into adulthood, while observing that child become self-reliant and a productive member of society has to rank high among the few joys of life.

As a pet lover throughout most of my life, I have often heard that "a dog is man's best friend." To a certain extent, I agreed, until I became a father. I used to enjoy taking my son for walks, teaching him how to play tennis, baseball, basketball, soccer, football, cards, checkers, chess, and how to fish. As he grew older, he became my fishing partner and we share many memories about our fishing trips.

Even though my knowledge was quite limited, I took great pride in trying to teach my son what I knew about the rudiments of auto mechanics, primarily because it was time we shared together.

I also tried to establish and maintain an environment which would allow my son to feel free to talk openly and freely with me about any subject of his concern. I can recall numerous times, after my son arrived home from school, he would tell me about his day's activities, and I would always try to listen attentively.

While writing about fatherhood, I asked my 21 year old son to share his opinions and describe me as a father. He wrote the following:

"My Dad is really old-fashioned and I have lots of respect for him. Sometimes my views and his are not always the same because I am part of the young generation.

I know my Dad doesn't understand some of my ways, but he's always there to listen and give me advice. Although, I admit that sometime I did not listen. You know, do my own thing.

When I was younger, there were situations, which caused me not to think clearly. I had to step back and look at my problems from a different perspective so I could make better decisions. My Dad taught me how to do that, along with many other things.

M y Dad is a real hard worker and that is how he survived in life. It has rubbed off on me, which is why I am excelling in life also.

After I graduated from high school and ventured out into the world, that is when I appreciated my dad's talks, lectures, and etc. It is funny how it works out that way. Being an adult is filled with different challenges, whether at work or everyday living. I am learning that it is important to have a strong head on my shoulder. My Dad really does influence me, although I rarely mention it, he really does. The lessons that he has taught me will continue to be a major part of my life because I want to be a survivor just like my Dad.

Being a father is a big responsibility, which some men seem unable to carry out. A father has to be understanding, caring and support his children, by letting them know that he is there for them on good days and the bad ones. A father also needs to give a child space and teach a child how to be independent. A father is really important in a child's life, that's why you can't half step when fatherhood comes along. Bottom line, any man can plant the seed, but only a real man can help that seed blossom into a respectable human being."

D. Michael Brown (2001)

In October 1989, I gave a talk at a reception honoring Bishop Curtis Mourning, pastor of the Gospel Temple Community Church in Bridgeport, Connecticut. My wife Deborah, and D. Michael accompanied me. On our way back home, after the reception, I asked D.Michael who was sitting in the back seat of the car, if he had listened to my speech. He said, "Yes." I asked if he understood my message. He said, "Yes." So I asked him to tell me what I said. D. Michael narrated my entire speech, almost verbatim. He was ten years old. I was quite impressed. Almost as impressed as I am about his written opinions about fatherhood. Most of all, I am proud of him, as "my son" and as the man he is growing to become.

After reading my son's hand written opinions about fatherhood, we had a frank and personal discussion. His views encouraged me to interview other men about their opinions on fatherhood.

My interview focused on three questions:

1). Describe your relationship with your father?

2). Describe your relationship with your child/child-
       ren?

3). What advice would you offer young men con-
       templating fatherhood?

Most of the men interviewed, indicated that their fathers played a significant role in their lives. Many believed that their lives would not have been as successful had their fathers not been a part of their growing up.

There appear to be a close correlation between the men who had a positive relationship with their fathers and the emotional bond they had developed with their own children.

Only two out of the initial seventeen respondents described a non-existent or negative relationship with their fathers. Nevertheless, the two men that described growing up without their biological fathers, indicated that the painful reality of growing up without a father or a father figure had motivated them to build a strong emotional bond with their children.

In addition to the seventeen respondents to the questionnaire, as of this writing, there have been well over two hundred subsequent responses from men who wanted to share their personal views about fatherhood. Overall, the responses have been positive, and in favor of the existing studies about the importance of fatherhood.

In many of my lectures, I often share the following advice with men, "The day set aside for Father's Day is not just a day to celebrate 'good fathers,' but all fathers."

There are several versions regarding the origin of Father's Day. Some say it began in 1908, during a church sermon in West, Virginia. Others say, it was first celebrated in 1915, by Harry Meek, president of the Chicago Lion's Club.

The version most widely accepted, however, is the belief that Father's Day first occurred in Spokane, Washington, by a woman named Sonora Louise Smart Dodd. It is widely believed that she thought of the idea for celebrating fathers while listening to a Mother's Day sermon in 1909. Her father, William Jackson Smart raised her and five siblings alone, after her mother died. Mrs. Dodd's efforts to honor her father and express her gratitude led to the first Father's Day celebration on June 19, 1910, the month of her father's birthday.

In 1924, the idea of a national Father's Day, received the attention of President Calvin Coolidge, which many believed help advanced the idea of a day to honor fathers.

In 1966 President Lyndon B. Johnson signed a presidential proclamation declaring the third Sunday of June as an official Father's Day. But, not until 1972, did Father's Day finally gain annual recognition and was established as a permanent national day of observance by a presidential proclamation.

Today, Father's Day is celebrated annually, nationally, and throughout many parts of the world. Nevertheless, in an effort for men around the world to counteract the negative image associated with fatherhood, it is imperative that all fathers play a more active and nurturing role in the lives of their children. It would increase their self-esteem and self-worth, as well as build confidence in their future generations.

From a personal point of view, the greatest joy and inspiration a man can receive during his life time is when he shares his life with a woman who acknowledges him with love, admiration, and respect. In addition to being blessed with a child/children who makes you feel as though you are his or her greatest hero.

A suggestion for all of the men who are allowed or have the opportunity to be fathers is to honor your commitment and responsibilities as one of the greatest joys of your life time. If you do this well, you will leave a proud legacy.

In regards to the question on immortality, my answer to all fathers is based on a borrowed quote from my sister Mrs. Lois Prime, that "children are our future and should be viewed as an infinite heir of our inner self" and ultimately as an extension of our lifeline for eternity.

Chapter VII

NOTES ON FAMILY
(A collection of short stories)

Throughout my professional career, I have lectured about the benefits of a nurturing family. Because all human beings are initially dependent on human interaction, the family serves as a primary unit for meeting the fundamental needs for love, acceptance, approval, warmth, security, and protection. It is within a family structure that most individuals develop a sense of self-identity. I have long maintained the belief and said repeatedly, that the family is the foundation of a true democracy and continues to be one of the best institutions for producing responsible and productive citizens.

Occasionally, during a few of my lectures, I was asked questions about how family values affect an individual's physical and emotional growth. I have also been asked whether an individual's potential to succeed or fail in life was based primarily on the influence of one's family values and relationships, or on one's ability to learn and adjust to standards of society. Such questions led to my interest in writing short stories about the impact of family life on the development of individual personality.

As a young social worker during the 1970s, I became familiar with many of the contemporary theories about family systems and methods of effective treatment.

Aside from the obvious clinical textbook cases on family therapy and various methods of treatment, most books and articles on family life focused attention on clinical research data and its findings. As a result, families were most often classified as normal or dysfunctional.

For this chapter, *NOTES ON FAMILY*, I will share a few of the short stories I have written over the years, about the dynamics of the family as a social institution. These are stories about different types of families using fictitious names, places, and events. These stories illustrate how external and internal influences impact families. It was also my intentions to reflect how different family values and relationships can influence an individual's life—attitude, behavior, and decisions.

The case of Mrs. Eable Humbrick

Mrs. Humbrick was 24 years old when she arrived in the United States of America from the West Indies. She was married and the mother of two daughters, Pauline, age six, and Sarah, age four. Mrs. Humbrick had been abandoned by her husband in Jamaica and left alone to raise the children without any visible means of financial support. She decided to accept employment as a cook at a hotel in New York, which also provided free board and lodging.

Mrs. Humbrick's employment did not include accommodations for her children, so she left her daughters in Jamaica, with an older sister. An agreement was made that the children would live with their aunt until Mrs. Humbrick could afford to make arrangements for her daughters to live with her in the United States.

From the low wages she earned, she regularly mailed a portion to her sister for the care of her daughters, and saved the balance. Seldom did she buy any personal items for herself. The uniform which her employment provided was frequently worn on her occasional day off. She was determined to be reunited with her children.

Several years passed before she was able to save enough money to afford an apartment and send for her teen-aged daughters.

While growing up on the island with their aunt, Pauline and Sarah attended school regularly. They had established friendship with many of their schoolmates, peers, and neighbors.

Sarah, the youngest daughter was excited about being reunited with her mother and was adjusting well to her new environment. The oldest daughter, 16 year old Pauline, was described as embittered and rebellious. She did not want to leave her aunt and friends, or move to the United States. Most of all, she did not want to leave her boyfriend and the life she had grown accustomed to on the island.

Within a short period of time, there were numerous acting out problems reported regarding Pauline's truancy from school, being disrespectful, staying out late at night, and refusing to obey her mother.

Pauline's involvement with law enforcement officials precipitated the need to initiate counseling for the first time in the family's history.

During the first two sessions with a court appointed social worker, Mrs. Humbrick arrived alone and was allowed to vent her frustrations. She talked about her impoverished background, first marriage, being abandoned by her husband, moving to the United States and leaving her daughters behind. After securing an attorney who helped her obtain a divorce from her estranged husband, she remarried an American. Her second marriage required adjusting into a "blended family" with three stepchildren.

For the fourth scheduled session, Mrs. Humbrick arrived with Pauline, who appeared mature for her chronological age. It seemed difficult for Pauline to express her feelings of anger without using profanity and shouting. Her mother accused her of using drugs. Pauline admitted to experimenting with different drugs with her new boyfriend, whom she described as a "drug pusher," but said that she was not an addict.

Recognizing Mrs. Humbrick's quiet desperation, and thinking that Pauline might not return for another session, the social worker permitted the session to exceed the usual one-hour limit.

Pauline described feelings of abandonment. She believed that when her mother left her and Sarah behind with their aunt, she had abandoned them because she no longer wanted or loved them. At this point, Pauline shouted repeatedly, "We were abandoned by our own mother and father, because they didn't care anything about us!" This belief prevailed throughout her growing years and had swelled into a mound of anger, now directed towards her mother.

The social worker requested the mother and daughter to position their chairs to face each other. The social worker asked the daughter to calm down, stop shouting, and talk directly to her mother without the profanity. Pauline was asked to describe what she was feeling inside at that particular moment, and to tell her mother what she needed from her for their relationship to grow. The social worker requested the mother to listen to her daughter without interruption.

Looking directly at her mother, Pauline very eloquently, though emotionally charged, described how she grew up feeling unloved and rejected by her mother and father, and the embarrassment of having to constantly explain to her peers why her parents were not part of her life. Pauline, described how she experienced what she interpreted as love, from the attention of different boys, and talked about her relationship with a 21 year old boyfriend. At this point, both mother and daughter were crying and crying deeply.

Eventually, Mrs. Humbrick could no longer contain her emotions. She reached out, touched Pauline's hand and told her how much she loved her.

Mrs. Humbrick told her daughter that it pained her to leave her children behind. "My leaving, to find a better way of life was done out of love. So that one day I could be a better parent for you and Sarah." She said.

Mrs. Humbrick tried to describe the impoverished conditions that she confronted at the time, and said that she did not have any other options. To which, Pauline quickly responded, "But Ma, why did you have to leave us?" Before Mrs. Humbrick could answer, Pauline continued, "If you were poor and had nothing but bread and water, we would have survived Ma, and at least, we would have known that you loved us." Mrs. Humbrick embraced her daughter and said, "Honey, you and Sarah are more important to me than anything in my life. If it had not been for the two of you, I don't think I would have wanted to continue living. It was for you and Sarah that I worked so hard and had a reason to keep going. Honey, mama love you." While in a tight embrace, they rocked each other back and forth. Their crying became so intense that neither was able to talk, coherently.

Recognizing that there had been a connection, the social worker remained silent, and allowed them to continue without interference. That was Mrs. Humbrick and Pauline's first face to face conversation together without an interruption from other family members, since their reunion.

The social worker assessed the situation as an emotional break-through and the start for a nurturing mother/daughter relationship. Pauline was now amenable to regular weekly counseling.

A follow-up session was scheduled for two days later and once a week thereafter. Two weeks later, Pauline returned to school. Arrangements were made for her to attend summer school so she could start the next school year with her regular class and graduate along with her classmates. Four months later, after regular weekly counseling sessions, which included other family members, consistent reports of improved family interactions and communication, the case was closed. The social worker agreed to serve as a reference for Pauline's application to attend college.

This case serves as an illustrative example of how some families with limited resources have historically had to sacrifice their personal happiness, including separation from their loved ones, while trying to keep their family unit together.

The positive results of this illustrative example shows how a mother's commitment and a fragmented family support system helped an individual grow stronger and more productive, which also prevented the daughter from further self-destruction and a life of criminal behavior.

The case of Mr. Nathan Zelbron

In some families, individuals may live in the same household together, but still do not feel love or express any feelings of closeness for one another. Such families often resemble a close knit family unit because of their blood ties. Even though they do not share any common interest or concerns beyond their individual need for survival. An individual in such a family can grow up feeling extremely lonely and a deep sense of alienation.

Nathan Zelbron was born into such a family, in a small rural town in Alabama. He was the ninth child born to his mother, Issy Taylor, an unmarried mother who had her first child at the age of 13, and was a grandmother at the age of 28.

Miss Issy did not have a formal education or any employment experiences outside of her farming and domestic chores. Her two oldest sons were serving time in an Alabama prison. One for stealing a pack of cigarettes, and the other for "running numbers," a form of gambling in which bets are made on the results of various types of sports or pari-mutuel totals.

As a little boy, Nathan was never allowed to cry or express any of his childhood fears and anxieties outwardly. Even at the age of five, one of his brothers or uncles would tell him that crying was for girls and sissies. The primary pattern of communication in his family involved shouting at each other, admonishing and controlling the children, with the use of physical punishment, if an adult or an older child believed it was necessary. There were no room for privacy, and individual creativity was often stifled by demands for conformity.

After Miss Issy's four daughters married and moved out, she decided to move up north. She took her three youngest children and four of her grand children with her. They moved into a one room efficiency, located in the inner-city of Chicago. She was able to locate employment as a maid during the day, and as a cocktail waitress at night, which meant leaving the children in the care of the oldest child.

Nathan's early childhood reflected dire poverty, which resulted in his dropping out of school at the age of nine, and working odd jobs to help provide for his large family. He described his boyhood days as filled with anger, sibling rivalry, lack of nurturing, and "every one for themselves" type of mentality. Living in the one-room efficiency, which was the only type of lodging his mother could afford, even with the added income from his employment. He had to sleep on the floor without a mattress, and if you were not in the room during meal time, you did not eat.

Nathan and the other children were mostly left alone for several hours, days, and sometimes for a week when their mother did not return home. The older children rarely assumed responsibility for the younger ones, and on a few occasions they also stayed away from the room until they moved out completely.

Growing up without having anyone nurture his childhood needs for recognition and approval, or always provide him with food when he was hungry. Nathan was forced to grow up without many of the basic needs that most children his age took for granted. No one took the time to teach him how to read or write, even though he was an extremely intelligent child. By fourth grade, he was reading on a seventh grade level. His childhood experiences was teaching him that he could not rely on others and that he had to learn how to manage by himself. He also recognized that the little money he earned from odd jobs was not enough to help take care of himself and his family.

At the age of 15, Nathan moved out and found employment with a construction company that provided temporary housing.

At the age of 16, he moved in with his 21 year-old girlfriend, Jade, whom was pregnant.

In the state of Illinois, at that particular time, males had to be at least 18 years-old to legally marry without parent consent. Females, however, could marry at the age of 16 with parent consent.

At 17, Nathan became the father of a healthy baby boy, whom he and Jade, named Nathan Zelbron Jr.

Once Nathan became the legal age of 18, he married his girlfriend, Jade.

Less than a year after they were married, Nathan and Jade separated.

Growing up without a positive male role model or father figure, Nathan did not have a clue about being a husband or father, beyond his desire to be a good provider. In an effort to compensate for his neglected youth, after paying the rent and buying the groceries, he spent most of his money on cars, motorcycles, clothing, and gambling.

Losing his wife and son forced Nathan to examine his life, although he did not understand why his wife left him. He was hurt emotionally, but his masculine pride would not allow him to share his feelings with anyone. He decided to turn his life around, by refusing to follow in the foot steps of any of the negative role models from his past. He stopped gambling, drinking, smoking, and absolutely refused to use drugs of any kind. He strongly believed that using drugs was a weakness, which would only lead to failure. He simply tried to block out his painful memories and emotions by becoming a hard worker.

Although, Nathan was a member of a large family and lived in a large metropolitan area, he did not have a social or family support system. Nobody seemed concerned about him, his marital problems, nor the loss of his child.

Feeling alone and isolated with his problems, Nathan accepted a job working as a crew member on a barge, drilling oil in Alaska. At five-feet-seven, Nathan was viewed as a "short man" compared to the other men working on the barge, but he was also recognized as one of the hardest working men on the shift. He started earning a salary higher than he had ever imagined. Within two years of working seasonally on the barge, he earned over $100,000.00 a year salary. Despite his lack of a proper education, he saved his income wisely.

He regularly mailed money to his wife and mother, although he never received a letter or response from either.

After seven years of consistent employment, he returned to Chicago, discovered that the money he had been mailing to his mother was used to supply her drug addiction. He also learned that two of his nieces had been placed into foster care. He was unable to locate his wife and child. Most of his recent letters had been returned without a forwarding address. He heard rumors that his wife had moved out of state with her boyfriend. Because he did not know how to search for his wife and child, he just buried his feelings, and spent most of his time working.

A few years later, Nathan decided to use part of his savings to start a small, unlicensed business, as a handyman. Unaware of the law, and believing that his wife's abandonment meant that they were no longer married, Nathan decided to marry for a second time.

At the age of 29, he married 33 year old Bertha Talbot, an independent, hard working, and christian woman. She was an elementary education schoolteacher, a part-time music instructor, and choir director for her church.

Bertha family's history could be traced back to the early 17th century. Her father, grandfather, great grandfather, and great-great-grandfather were Methodist ministers. Her great-great-grandfather was a pioneer and one of the co-founders of the African Methodist Episcopal (AME) Church, which grew out of the April1816 convention held in Philadelphia, Pennsylvania.

Bertha was the youngest of five offsprings born to her parents. Her father was the family's church pastor and a strict disciplinarian. Her mother was a housewife and primary caretaker of the family. She was also very active in the activities of her church and community. Bertha grew up feeling loved and a strong sense of attachment towards her family.

She was a woman of high moral character who had always lived her life above reproach. When she announced her engagement, some of her close friends criticized her decision to marry a "high school drop-out." They believed that a woman with a master's degree in education could never be happily married to a man with less education. Bertha's closest friends, however, were less judgmental and expressed their congratulations.

During their courtship, Bertha discovered that Nathan was a complex and difficult man, who was "set in his ways," with simple and old-fashioned values, much of which were compatible with her values. She viewed Nathan as a kind, thoughtful, and generous man. More importantly, she believed that he loved her and wanted to make her happy.

Bertha was a motivating and inspiring woman. She could find something good in everyone. Most people felt an urge to be their very best when in her presence. She taught Nathan how to improve his reading, writing, and comprehension skills. She encouraged him to apply for a contractor's license and start his own construction company.

Initially, most of Nathan's customers were members of Bertha's church, where she also served on the board of trustees. A few years after opening his business, Nathan gained financial success and hired several employees.

Nathan had always been a loner and worrywart who found it difficult to trust others. He used silence as a defense mechanism to shield his insecurities. It was not unusual for him to work 12 or 14 hours per day. He could perform almost any manual task to perfection, but, whenever he felt overwhelmed with stress, he would worry away at his problems.

Nathan's inability to comprehend social, legal, and business expectations, or what he referred to as "Too much fistication and technology to just do my job," caused intense anxiety.

It seemed ironic that Nathan, who was known for his quiet demeanor, would become argumentative when he felt distressed, which was typical of the style of communication he grew up with as a child. Whereas, Bertha, known for her loquaciousness, was always calm under pressure. She preferred to think, reason, and discuss a situation before making a decision. Due to her strong faith, she believed, no matter what happens it will turn out okay.

If Nathan was unable to get away or avoid Bertha so he could worry in silence about what he viewed as a complicated problem, he would act out his anxious feelings.

Whenever Nathan becomes enraged or gets into one of his acting-out moods, which Bertha called "fussin fits," she would kneel and pray. This often leaves Nathan arguing by himself, which also ends the argument.

Nathan asked Bertha, why she always pray when he tries to talk to her about his problems. "That is not talking, especially when you're in one of your moods of putting yourself down." She said. "I pray for you because I know you have an ache in your heart, which only God can heal."

Because of Nathan's occasional nervous acting-out behavior, an outsider listening to him could easily think they had a dysfunctional relationship or that he was an abusive person. But Bertha knew him as a strong willed, but soft hearted, and generous man whom she believed had never reconciled the demons of his mind developed from his childhood experiences. The only person she had ever seen or heard Nathan hurt was himself because most of his verbiage was self-recriminating.

Bertha's consistent behavior encouraged Nathan to start taking positive actions towards resolving his own conflicts, rather than just imagining and fearing the worst scenarios. Her efforts helped Nathan become a little less dramatic in his way of speaking and acting when he felt stressed. He also hired a legal adviser, bookkeeper, and an accountant for his business, which reduced his level of stress, tremendously.

In addition to being tolerant of his behavior, increasingly, Nathan was discovering Bertha to be the best friend he had ever had in his life. Bertha became the first person he allowed himself to trust, to a certain extent. Although Nathan's behavioral reaction to his work environment was less dramatic, he continued to be a workaholic who struggled with anxiety and depression. He lived in constant fear that he would lose control of everything he had worked so hard to establish, including his marriage. His anxieties prevented him from enjoying his success. Because he did not trust doctors, he refused to seek medical attention regarding his constant thoughts and recurring dreams about death and dying.

Bertha was four years older than Nathan. She believed that she would never be blessed with children, but at the age of 34, she gave birth to a healthy baby girl named Natalie.

Nathan rebuffed his wife's efforts to make him a nurturing father. He refused to hold his infant daughter, fearing that he might be too rough and hurt her. Two years later, they were blessed with the birth of a second child, a son named Nathaniel. Nathan loved his wife and children, but he maintained the belief that nurturing children was a woman's role and being a good provider was what made a man a good father.

After receiving several successive bids for multi-million dollar construction contracts, Nathan's hard work, along with the support and guidance from his wife made him a millionaire.

He gained public respect and a reputation as a community leader when Mayor Harold Washington appointed him chairman of a community/business task force, which led to building modern housing and businesses in urban areas.

Because Nathan spent most of his childhood working, he had never played baseball or any other sports. When the Chicago White Sox recruited him to co-sponsor the little league baseball team in his community, he felt so honored by the request that, to his own surprise, he signed up for a three week baseball camp to learn about baseball from a professional player.

Mr. Nathan Zelbron's "rags to riches" economic status aroused public interest. His name, picture, and story appeared in several magazines, newspapers, and were broadcast on numerous local television stations. One day, he received a registered certified letter from his first wife's attorney. Jade was suing him for divorce, alimony, and back child support payments.

Bertha was totally unaware of her husband's previous marriage, which made their marriage illegal.

Nathan was arrested and charged with bigamy, which was considered a felony. He was immediately released on bail, due to the fact that his first wife had deserted him, and based on the number of years of separation, but he had to pay a hefty fine and several thousands of dollars to his first wife. This incident led to a reunion with Nathan Jr., his first born son, who was in jail for selling drugs.

After Nathan Jr. was released, he agreed to live and work with his father.

Nathan taught his son how to weld different metals together, how to read blueprints, and how to use and repair machines and tools. He also offered Nathan Jr., a permanent position in his construction company. Their working together made them feel less like strangers as they learned more about each other and improved their father/son relationship. The influence of living an orderly and structured life, while observing the academic, social, and cultural achievements of his half-brother and sister, helped changed Nathan Jr.'s lifestyle, and ultimately his life.

Nathan and Bertha recognized Natalie and Nathaniel as perfect children who made them feel proud at home, in school, and at church. Both grew up doing their household chores, participated in church activities, and made good grades in school without conflict or any disciplinary problems.

Natalie wanted to become a schoolteacher, and Nathaniel, a construction engineer with hopes of expanding his father's business.

Nathan's situation, however, had created a family crisis and a marital rift between him and Bertha, who demanded that they remarry following his divorce from Jade.

Bertha felt betrayed by his lack of trust in her and not confiding in her earlier about his marital status. She felt ashamed in front of her neighbors and church members. She believed she had been living a life of sin and others viewed her as a fraud. It was considered an abomination that her children were officially born out-of-wedlock. She stopped attending church. Some days, she refused to get out of bed while spending the majority of her time watching sermons on the Christian television networks, until she initiated counseling.

Nathan refused to attend counseling with Bertha, but supported her decision to seek professional help.

After settling his divorce matters, Nathan and Bertha remarried in a small, private, and civil ceremony. Bertha continued her involvement with individual counseling for two years, which she believed enabled her to overcome the stress and public embarrassment. She returned to church where she was greeted with a tremendously warm, loving, and prayerfully reception.

In addition to the support of her church and prayers, Bertha, credited counseling with helping her maintain her marriage with Nathan, whom she described as "a good man, a good husband, and an excellent father, but a very stubborn man."

Late one evening, one of Nathan's sisters telephoned him for their mother who had returned to Alabama to live after developing AIDS. Nathan told Bertha, who answered the telephone, to tell his sister that he was not at home. He was still harboring years of deep seated feelings of anger towards his mother for his troubled childhood. He refused to talk to his mother, even though Bertha was gesturing vigorously and insisting that he should accept her call. Nathan rationalized his decision with the belief that his mother only called when she wanted more money. Bertha disagreed, but he adamantly refused.

About two-thirty in the morning, Nathan's sister telephoned again. She reported that their mother died four hours after her first call.

The enormous guilt that Nathan experienced was the situation that led him to willingly attend the next three years of his life in psychotherapy. Unlike his previous bouts of depression, after hearing about his mother's death, he became catatonic and had to be admitted into the hospital.

After years of ignoring his inner feelings, Nathan's first hurdle in therapy involved helping him become more communicative and trusting. In order for his therapy to be effective, he had to openly and freely trust his therapist by sharing all of his pent up feelings and emotions, which he had always believed was unmanly to reveal.

Nathan described his three years of therapy as his "growing years." He discovered how his childhood experiences influenced his attitudes, behavior, and decisions. He was learning how to view life and other people from a positive perspective. In addition to his therapy, Bertha insisted on Nathan reading a scripture from the Bible with her every morning before leaving for work, at meal time, and before going to bed.

For the first time in his life, Nathan was baptized, and started attending church regularly on Sundays with his family. He started participating in family social activities and talking to his children about some of his childhood experiences. He took the time to listen to the details of their daily activities, rather than use his overwhelming work schedule as an excuse to avoid such discussions.

Nathan realized that the nurturing he missed during his childhood was being amply supplied by his wife and his three children. By allowing himself the freedom to enjoy the love and devotion from his family, church members, and newly established close friends, he said that for the first time in his life, he felt like a real human being and part of a larger society.

Nathan and Bertha taught Natalie, Nathaniel, and Nathan Jr. the importance of education, hard work, and responsibility. They also taught them how to respect themselves and the rights of others. Nathan was proud of the fact that he raised his children without using corporal punishment. In retrospect, he believed that the abuse he suffered during his childhood had made him determined to raise his children with patience, understanding, and love. He loved his children and there did not exist any doubts in his mind that they loved him.

Nathan decided to change the name of his construction company. He ordered new signs to reflect a father/son family business relationship, which was his way of expressing his appreciation to Nathan Jr.

Bertha was responsible for planning and organizing the grand opening event. The ceremony was well attended by many of her close friends and church members. In many ways, it was also Bertha's coming out party, to acknowledge that she was a woman of faith, and no longer grieving, or living with shame.

During the presentation of the new signs and the ribbon cutting ceremony for the opening of a new and larger building, Nathan praised Bertha and his family. He thanked his wife for saving his life. For the ceremonial toast, he said, "I was born in rough waters, but God smooth the waves by blessing me with all of you."

The case of Margaret Catherine Hill

Margaret Catherine was a distinguish looking woman who looked much older than her stated age. She seemed anxious to talk about her life story. She was born in England, the largest and most populous island of the United Kingdom of Great Britain. At the time of her birth, her parents, Lord Ludshire, and Elizabeth Ashton Osbourne, known to her acquaintances as "Lady Ludshire," were active members of the well established London, England society, and the Church of England.

Lord Ludshire was a graduate of the University of Oxford, and a wealthy industrialist.

At a very early age, Margaret established an emotional attachment to her doting father, who absolutely adored her. She was his only heir. She never felt close to her mother who appeared jealous of her relationship with her father. When Lord Ludshire was away on business, Margaret was always left in the custody of a full time nanny. Her mother was too busy for a little tot. Lady Ludshire preferred to spend her time attending societal functions and planning tea parties for the established elite.

As a young girl, Margaret enjoyed the lifestyle of a princess. She had a private chauffeur, tutor, nanny, cook, and a social calendar. Her father took her to Buckingham Palace, she attended lawn parties at 1 Downing Place, and regularly played with other children of royalty.

Following the advent of new technology, a drastic change in the European economy, industrial inefficiency, and other social and political conflicts, the family's business went bankrupt. Lord Ludshire blamed himself and committed suicide. It was Margaret who found his body in his study.

Lady Ludshire was unable to cope with the shame and humiliation of her husband's suicide. She suffered an emotional break down and was sent to an asylum.

After discovering her father's body, losing her mother, and her nanny, Margaret was not offered any form of psychotherapy or counseling. Instead, she was left on her own to resolve her problems. It was believed that she was young and would outgrow any memory or emotional disturbance of her family's tragedy. At the age of ten, Margaret was sent to a private preparatory boarding school. Later, at the age of 16, she was sent to a private women's college.

Margaret described her childhood, following the death of her father, as one with strict discipline and rigorous daily routines without any positive emotional attachments. Her days were spent with academic studies of arts, sciences, and languages. In addition to piano lessons, ballet, and etiquette.

At the age of 19, before completing her college education Margaret was notified in writing of her mother's death. She had not seen her mother since the age of 10. Even though she was the only known relative, she did not receive the notice until several months after the funeral. As the sole heir, the notice also informed that the Ludshire's estate had been depleted and could no longer afford to support her.

Margaret accepted a job as a librarian. During her spare time, she traced her family's history. That was when she read about how her family had been decimated by mental illness and politics. Her family's history could be traced back to the early part of the Middle Ages–a period in European history between Antiquity and the Renaissance, which is widely known as the "Dark Ages."

She discovered that her father had 15 generations of schizophrenia and suicide in his family's genealogy. Her father, grand father, and great grandfather, were born with primogeniture (first-born right of inheritance). Her father's upper class ancestry could be traced over three centuries of hereditary nobility.

Her paternal great grandfather served in the lower house of parliament, known as the House of Commons, where he reportedly committed suicide following a political scandal. His only son (Margaret's grandfather), shied away from politics in an effort to recapture his family's good name and reputation. He tried to regain his family's prestige by concentrating on managing the family's oil corporations and textiles industry. His refusal to serve in the House of Lords, however, was viewed as an affront to the established political elite. Rumors were spread about misappropriation of funds and poor labor practices in the family's business, which led to her grandfather's death (suicide).

The historical documents, magazines and newspaper articles that Margaret read indicated that her father assumed the family's business at a low ebb and a time when the established political structure did not want the family's business to succeed. It was her mother who used her social connections and political persuasion to help her husband with the political network. But the inevitable decline had already begun. Her father was forced to file bankruptcy, and the government took over their family's business.

Margaret concluded that the same people who created controversy about the alleged corporate scandals that destroyed her father also wanted to harm her.

With the belief that her family's name had been disgraced, and that she had a definite genetic predisposition for mental illness, she decided to disavow herself from her family's history by moving to America to start a new life.

Although, Margaret had not completed her college education, she had acquired a well rounded education. She was fluent in four languages, English, French, Italian, and German. She also had a thorough knowledge of the arts and sciences.

She avoided applying for the higher level diplomatic positions, which she was amply qualified, because those positions required a thorough background check. During her employment search, she was offered an administrative position in the State's Bureau of Public Affairs, or to become an administrative assistant to the Under Secretary for Public Diplomacy and Public Affairs. She declined both. In an effort to protect her privacy, she only sought mid-level routine employment, which often place her in unfamiliar environments.

In America, she was quickly hired as an interpreter. Despite her employment skills, she found it difficult to work in a crowded office, especially around other women. Because Margaret never felt close to her mother and was unable to develop any type of emotional bond with any of the women at the private schools she attended, she found it easier to relate to males.

The emotional trauma Margaret experienced during her childhood, also made it difficult for her to function without intense anxiety and mood disorders. Filled with self doubts, she avoided social contacts and activities because she suspected that anyone allowed to get close to her would discover her family's secret, or develop the belief that she might be insane, and try to destroy her. It seemed as though, the more she tried to behave in a manner she thought most people considered "normal," to protect her secret, the more others around her viewed her as peculiar.

At five-feet-nine, Margaret was recognized as a naturally beautiful and stylish woman with impeccable class, which made her immediately noticeable under any and all circumstances. Despite her continuing efforts to conceal her royal heritage, her aristocratic upbringing revealed her elegance and sophistication. Nevertheless, whenever she was in a crowd or around female co-workers, her over anxious, over sensitive, and obsessive behavior prevented her from exhibiting her natural charm and poise. In stressful situations, her behavior reflected an histrionic personality disorder—an over dramatic reaction or way of talking. In an effort to control her behavior during working hours, she avoided talking to her coworkers.

She was not experienced at engaging in trite conversations. She had never been grocery shopping, or ever had to do her own laundry or house cleaning. She could not relate to conversations about television soap operas, nor the typical family's social and financial conflicts. When she tried to relate to some of her co-workers, she often appeared as out-of-touch with common everyday reality, or not having any common sense. A few of her co-workers interpreted her unexplained behavior as apathetic and snobbish.

Margaret's inability to get along with some of the less sophisticated female co-workers led to several office conflicts, resulting in her leaving or being fired from highly paid jobs, including her employment as a diplomatic specialist in foreign affairs, which resulted from an internal office promotion.

After exhausting several lucrative employment opportunities, she located a job as a bi-lingual secretary in an immigration office. She was the only female on the staff. This became her longest held employment.

One of the men in the office provided her with daily transportation to and from work because he lived in the same direction as her apartment and she did not have a driver's license. They developed a romantic relationship, which led to marriage. Their marriage was void of any out-side social activities. Margaret refused to socialize with any of their neighbors, or her husband's friends, or family members. Two months after their divorce, Margaret quit her job at the immigration office.

Later, Margaret met Patrick Heeney Sucat, described as a traveling salesman on a diplomatic mission from Ireland. She felt comfortable with Patrick, because he did not make any social demands on her, nor did he appear interested in having her meet any of his acquaintances. He appeared to cherish privacy as much as she did.

After their first date, whenever Patrick was in America on business he stayed in Margaret's apartment. A few months after their initial meeting, they married and later had two children.

During their marriage, Patrick continued traveling between Ireland and America. Increasingly, during his short business trips to America, their relationship became cold and unresponsive. After five years of marriage, he filed for a divorce and returned to Ireland, without provid-ing any financial support for Margaret or his children. After petitioning the courts in America for unpaid child support payments, she discovered how very little she knew about her husband. She was unable to locate him in Ireland. All she knew was what little he told her. Patrick told her that he was a descendant of royalty. That his grandfather and an uncle were members of Oireachtas (Parliament), and other members of his family served in the Seanad (the senate).

As a former librarian, she researched information, but were unable to find anything about the Heeney or Sucat family that related to Patrick. Since she was familiar with international protocol, she contacted the embassy in Dublin, the United Nations, and other foreign affairs departments.

She discovered that the Patrick Sucat, whom she married was an unemployed swindler with an assumed name, which he used to conceal his criminal past. She also discovered that she was not the first woman he had married and abandoned with children. Fearful of exposing her royal identity and the past she so desperately wanted to leave behind, she decided not to pursue her investigation. Feeling as though she could not forget or forgive her ex-husband for his betrayal and abandoning her and his children she became overwhelmed with hatred, anger, and bitterness, which caused her to feel ill and miss numerous days from work.

After obtaining and losing a few more jobs with perfunctory titles, she decided to auction off her remaining heirlooms to defray some of the incurred housing and living expenses. She was forced to make additional changes in her lifestyle, and for the first time in her life she had to live without the services of a maid.

After depleting all of her resources, she was evicted from her luxury town house apartment. Her low income and status as a single parent qualified her for public housing.

Margaret did not have a support system of friends or family ties. She was self-involved and had little capacity to give warmth, affection, or establish an emotional bond, even with her own children. She did, however, make sure her children were properly fed, sent to school, and wore clean clothes. In her own way, she loved her children and they loved her, but she found it extremely difficult to hug or express her maternal instincts, which she denied having. The anxiety of going to work everyday and taking care of her children consumed her energy.

While living in the housing project, she met Mr. Warren Hill, a janitor, whom she observed to be a polite man that never made her feel inadequate. Mr. Hill was the only member of the housing project personnel that she felt comfortable enough to allow inside of her apartment for repairs and maintenance. She believed other staff members were either criminals or spies from the British government who wanted to harm her.

One day, Mr. Hill spent most of his working hours inside her apartment. At least three hours were spent searching for a microphone, which she believed had been hidden by the Central Intelligence Agency (CIA).

Mr. Hill did not understand her behavior, but he liked the attention, flattery, and other expressions of gratitude, which he interpreted as respect and admiration.

Intellectually, they had very little, if anything, in common, but she was lonely and enjoyed his company. She considered his calm and unpretentious behavior, albeit self-deprecating, to be saintly compared to the obnoxious behavior of the married men at her job who flirted with her constantly.

Margaret made frequent requests for Mr. Hill to come to her apartment for various repairs, which led to a romantic relationship. Her two children also liked Mr. Hill, who regularly took them to recreational parks, movies, fast food restaurants, and places their mother refused to take them. When Margaret became pregnant, Mr. Hill was ecstatically overjoyed about becoming a father and asked her to marry him.

At the age of 42, this was Mr. Hill's first marriage. He had been employed with the public housing department since the age of 25. He came from a very large family that felt proud to see him finally get married and settle down.

Throughout the pregnancy, members of Mr. Hill's family visited Margaret and offered their assistance. They consistently invited her and the children to participate in family activities, but Margaret persisted in her refusal.

Mr. Hill's family were ordinary people who placed a

high priority on family life. They were confused by Margaret's rejection, but refused to give up trying to include her into the various family gatherings.

Mr. Hill loved Margaret. He believed that she was a gift from God, but her constant rejection of his family and refusal to go out in public with him created an embarrassing and frustrating situation. He was unable to explain his new wife's behavior beyond viewing it as a blow to his manhood and a rejection of his family. He felt trapped between his family's questions and his wife's demands to make his family leave her alone. At times, she appeared hysterical while screaming at him to stop his family from annoying her.

It was obvious to Mr. Hill that Margaret viewed his family's visits and invitations as unwanted stress, but he simply did not understand why or how to handle the situation. Margaret started focusing on the negative aspects of their marriage, which led to viewing Mr. Hill as an incompatible mate. She felt uncomfortable with the idea of confronting her husband with her new found reality, so she started withdrawing from any kind of intimacy with him as an emotional and non-verbal way of ending their marriage.

Before the birth of their child, Margaret requested a divorce and demanded that he move out of their apartment.

About four years after the divorce and birth of their child, Margaret complained to her supervisor about numbness, chest discomfort, and difficulty breathing. She collapsed at work. Due to her disorientation, trembling, sweating, and rapid heart beat while clinching her chest, her co-workers thought she was having a heart attack. After she was rushed to the hospital's emergency room, her condition was diagnosed as a panic attack. Further medical examinations also revealed that she had a terminal illness.

In addition to her usual anxiety disorders, she felt emotionally distraught over her illness and concerned about the future of her children. Before terminating her employment, the employee assistance program referred her to the state's social services department. A state social worker was assigned to her case, to assist her in meeting her medical care needs and plans for her children's future.

Mr. Hill was contacted by the assigned social worker, since no other names of relatives were listed in the hospital's records. Mr. Hill agreed to meet with the social worker to discuss how he could participate in the planning for the children's future. He had remarried and started a new family, but expressed a willingness to cooperate, including adopting the children.

With Margaret's permission, Mr. Hill attended all of the scheduled family counseling sessions held in her apartment.

The social worker was encouraged by the positive feelings of concern expressed among each family member after they were able to get pass the anger, denial, resentment, and hopelessness. Not only did the family discussions and planning focus on the children's future, but also on providing better health care, assistance, and maintenance for Margaret.

Each family member, including Mr. Hill, assumed a role in following up with medical appointments, prescriptions, and supervising a planned diet. Arrangements were made for an outside health care agency to provide ongoing home health care.

Mr. Hill, played a very active role in the children's daily lives. He started visiting more frequently, sharing time with them at their mother's apartment and at his home. He did not make any distinction between the children. He and his family treated them all the same, as though they were all his biological children. He also ran several errands for the children's mother and occasionally spent time just talking to her about her medical activities.

The children felt empowered by their acceptance from Mr. Hill's family, and observing their mother and father behave as though they had become close friends. One could readily feel the optimistic change in the children's home atmosphere.

Medications and psychotherapy were used to treat Margaret's anxiety disorders, which allowed her to live without delusions or the constant fear of being harmed, and the frightening voices of hallucination that warned her of ever-present danger.

Follow up medical examinations indicated a slight improvement in Margaret body's response to her less stressful environment and health care services. There was also an improved response to her new medication.

Receiving professional counseling and psychiatric treatment for the first time, allowed Margaret to talk about her childhood trauma and gain an understanding of her behavior. It also allowed her to tear down emotional barriers. Finally, Mr. Hill gained an understanding of his ex-wife's fear and anxieties. Margaret developed a close and trusting relationship with one of Mr. Hill's sisters who regularly prepared meals and provided child care for the children during frequent doctor's visits.

Supportive services led to a renewed sense of hope for improvement, which replaced her feelings of despair, isolation, and hopelessness.

By employing effective family therapy techniques, the social worker made a positive contribution and a difference in this family's relationships. The social worker also proved how much a family's involvement, commitment, and love could become an effective form of therapy.

The case of Mr. Anthony Tavis

Anthony Tavis was born in New Jersey, reared by his mother, Janet, and an older sister, Anna Marie. Anthony did not know his father or his whereabouts. He did not feel comfortable asking his mother about his biological father, because the few times he made inquiries, his mother refused to answer his questions and became visibly upset with him. His mother never mentioned his father, beyond telling him once that he looked just like his father.

Janet Tavis was an entrepernuer. She owned a restaurant, which occupied the first floor of her two-story home. Janet, Anthony, and Anna Marie lived on the second floor. The restaurant was located near a major highway, opened twenty-four hours, seven days a week, including holidays. A gas service station and truck stop located across the street provided regular customers for breakfast, lunch, dinner, and snacks for late night travelers.

Anthony and Anna Marie were half-brother and sister. Anna Marie was nine years older and resented having the responsibility of looking after her brother.

When Anna Marie was younger, she was regularly left upstairs alone, or in the care of one of her mother's boyfriends, until she reported being molested. Her mother dismissed her accusation as a cry for more attention. Anna Marie felt neglected by her mother and was jealous of any attention Anthony received from their mother or her biological father during his infrequent visits.

Anna Marie frequently reminded Anthony that he was not her real brother and would taunt him by telling him that he was adopted. She pretended that she was glad to grow up without much adult supervision, and allowed to have authority over Anthony, although she also expressed a great deal of anger and resentment. Anna Marie was verbally, emotionally, and physically abusive towards Anthony. She often threatened further abuse if he told their mother.

Anna Marie pushed Anthony down a flight of stairs, which broke his left arm, when he was nine years old. He had to be rushed to the hospital's emergency room. Anthony told his mother and doctors that he fell. After his release from the hospital, Anna Marie burned him with a cigarette, because he almost got her into trouble. At the age of nineteen, Anna Marie had a baby, married, and moved out of the home.

Janet was a workaholic who struggled with bouts of depression, especially when business was slow and she was unable to work. Her work and status as an entrepernuer were her primary source of income and pleasure. Her employment was a constant reason for not participating in any of Anthony's activities and interests. She also seemed unaware of his immature and withdrawn behavior. As long as he conformed to the rules, expectations, and did not cause any problems at home or school, which would demand taking time away from her restaurant, Janet assumed he was growing up as a normal child. Even his obesity was viewed as being a healthy child. She believed that leaving Anna Marie to take care of Anthony when he was younger, prevented her from being labeled as a neglectful parent.

In elementary and high school, Anthony displayed various signs of anti-social behavior. He felt uncomfortable around people, withdrew from large crowds, and preferred to be alone. Outside of his regular classroom activities, he only participated in school activities when forced to do so, as part of a class project.

Whenever he was forced into the company of others, he preferred to associate with the younger children whom he could 'boss' or 'control' rather than try to cope with the competitiveness of older children, or peers of his own age. Occasionally, he got into trouble for his passive aggressive behavior.

Anthony did not recall growing up with anyone expressing any form of affection towards him. He could not remember if his mother had ever given him a hug prior to his high school graduation, leaving home, and returning home for visits. When asked how his mother expressed her love while he was growing up. He said, "She would buy me things." He further elaborated, that when he reached the age of 16, his mother provided him with employment in her diner and taught him how to manage a business.

After graduating from high school, Anthony entered the military. Prior to his enlistment, Anthony had to present a copy of his birth certificate to the military recruiting officer. He had hoped it would reveal the name of his father, but he was sadly disappointed. At birth, he was delivered at home by a midwife. Only his mother's name appeared on the document. "Unknown" was typed for father's information. In high school, he heard rumors that his father had been a convict, connected to the mafia, and was killed during a war between rivaling families. Of course, Anthony had no way of confirming or denying the rumor and no one ever told him his father's name.

Not unlike many individuals with a troubled childhood, Anthony experienced numerous relationship conflicts. The strict regimen of the military system allowed him an opportunity to conceal his emotions, yet he encountered frequent problems with various military personnel.

Military life forced Anthony to make a few attitude and behavioral adjustments. During his first two years of service, he was constantly engaged in personality conflicts. There were complaints about his controlling behavior, manipulating others to carry out his work details, and showing little or no regards for the rights of others in his unit.

Unaware he was acting out unresolved emotional conflicts from his childhood, Anthony interpreted those complaints as an unfair effort to block his promotions to higher ranks. With the belief that he was always right and others were wrong, Anthony was motivated to succeed. With hard work and strong determination, he moved up in rank in rapid successions.

The structure of the military and his assigned duties helped him gain a sense of power and control. His authoritarian and aggressive personality gained him a great deal of respect from superior officers. Many of the recruited soldiers under his command however, viewed him as excessively tough, to the point of describing him as a ruthless bully. From Anthony's point of view, he was only performing his duty—turning boys into men.

The military taught him discipline and leadership skills. From the established chain of command he learned about accountability, management, setting goals and achieving them. He also learned about the importance of an efficient communication network.

After his 21 year career in the military, Anthony was unable to find work. He took a few college business courses and decided to start his own business. Anthony's authoritarian personality and shrewd business manipulations helped him become a wealthy entrepreneur. Unknowingly, his lack of interest in developing interpersonal relationships continued to serve as a shield to block others from getting to know him. Once again, he found himself acting out his frustrations and hostilities, which triggered intense reactions from many of his business associates and employees. The ones who were intimidated by his physical appearance, viewed him as frightening, a tough negotiator, and uncompromising in his business dealings. Most of his employees viewed him as detached, distant, and unapproachable. From his point of view, because he held his staff and business associates accountable, they accused him of being abrasive. He further believed that the reason they resented him and called him a "control freak" or con artist was because he was extremely knowledgeable.

Because Anthony had not experienced a relationship based on mutual love and an abiding concern, he was unable to understand how his behavior affected others. He was the owner of four hardware stores, two restaurants, and a coin operated laundromat. He had 143 full time employees, 17 part-time employees, and averaged about 10 million dollars in sales annually, yet he still felt alienated, alone, and lonely.

At the age of 47, Anthony was diagnosed with a swollen prostate. In the process of assessing his life, he feared that he would die before allowing himself to enjoy life, marry, or have children. He decided to enter counseling for the first time in his life. He requested counseling for "some middle-aged concerns."

Anthony's businesses were located in Washington, DC, but he made regular trips to New Jersey to visit his mother and sister. His mother was acknowledged as a positive force in his life and for his business success.

After her divorce, Anna Maria became an evangelist and was employed as a coordinator of a women's support program. He and Anna Marie never talked about their childhood, but tell others that they are close and love one another.

Anthony said that the military made a man out of him, taught him how to organize, plan for the future, and not "waste time" dwelling on the past. He believed that the only reason he was able to succeed in the business world was due to his ability to develop a positive attitude, rather than viewing life from a negative perspective, regardless of his childhood circumstances.

The fact that he never married or maintained a stable relationship became the focal point of his counseling. Anthony was encouraged to examine how his childhood trauma and repressed anger thwarted his social activities. Instead of pursuing a relationship or engaging in social activities that were not business related, he channeled his sexual and aggressive energy into building one success-ful business after another. Because his businesses took precedence, he rationalized that he never had time to develop a social life, other than occasional dates, includ-ing a few women whom he hired from an escort service. These women often accompanied him to various busi-ness conventions and for exposure during business trans-actions.

While confronting medical problems and rapidly approaching the age of 50, Anthony experienced a deep sense of regret and loneliness. He wished he had taken the time to search for a mate with whom he could share the remainder of his adult life.

As an eligible bachelor, Anthony could afford many of the luxuries of life, but subconsciously, his early childhood experiences made it difficult for him to develop a roman-tic or trusting relationship.

Over the years, Anthony had several social and busi-ness related dates. None of the women he dated seemed to satisfy his demanding personality or compensate for his earlier emotional deprivation. His dates ended with disappointment because they failed to meet his insatiable demands for love or idealized romantic fantasy. No mat-ter how responsive any of the women he dated were, he still found it difficult to believe that they were really in love with him. He often rationalized his feelings with the belief that they were only interested in his money and would eventually break his heart.

Anthony's therapy was designed to help him understand the origin of his personality conflicts, and to take a deeper look into his hidden feelings.

As a child, Anthony had learned how to suppress (to consciously hide) and repress (unconsciously hidden) his emotional pain and anger, and the memories associated with those feelings.

At six-feet-three, 235 pounds, Anthony had the physical appearance that many viewed as intimidating. He definitely exhibited a "Type A" behavior pattern, which refers to someone who is aggressive and impatient, compared to a "Type B" behavior pattern of someone described as relaxed or easy-going.

While trying to overcome his anxiety to talk about his childhood, he started connecting with his repressed thoughts and feelings, it was revealed that inside the rough exterior of this tough, well disciplined, and hardened military officer turned aggressive businessman was an emotionally wounded and frightened little boy with a fragile ego, who wanted very much to love, be loved, and understood.

In counseling, Anthony was encouraged to recognize how he had been controlled by his deep seated emotions, even though he thought he was in total control of his actions. He had to stop trying to control everyone and everything around him. His controlling behavior, need to always be right and others wrong was a way of lifting himself up while devaluing others. His therapy was helping him learn how to express his true inner feelings, cope with his fear of rejection, and allow himself to trust others with his feelings, even when he felt vulnerable.

Anthony continued talking openly about his painful childhood as he described how he had always denied or suppressed such memories to avoid feeling angry and out of control. As he continued talking, he started crying. It was a deep guttural cry. In his effort to stop crying, he wiped away the tears, looked at his therapist and said, "You must really think that I'm a wimp now." The therapist recognized that Anthony felt vulnerable and disappointed with himself for not controlling his emotions.

The therapist listen attentively as Anthony started talking boastfully about his knowledge of sports and interest in boxing. Anthony identified himself as somewhat of a boxing historian. He could trace boxing back to the bare-knuckle fighting of James Figg who in 1719 declared himself the first heavyweight champion, up to the current (1970s) bouts of Muhammad Ali.

Anthony appeared engrossed in his conversation about the greatest boxing legends of history. He believed that John Arthur "Jack" Johnson(1878-1946) was the most formidable fighter of his time, due to the political and social climate he had to contend against. In his opinion, the July 4, 1910 boxing match between Jack Johnson and James J. Jeffries (1875-1953) was one of the best fights recorded in boxing history. Although, Joseph Louis Barrow (1914-1981), known throughout the world as Joe Louis, the famous "Brown Bomber" was his all-time favorite.

Some of the excitement in Anthony's voice began to taper off about his love of sports. His voice lowered. "Someone said my father looked just like Joe Louis." He said.

Then, without the slightest provocation, he said, "You know, I have never used the words "I love you, nor has anyone ever told me that they loved me."

Recognizing that Anthony had hit another emotional

connection, his therapist assured him that by connecting with his inner emotions and his ability to release them, was not a sign of weakness, but a display of trust, courage, and a positive sign for his recovery.

Anthony finally realized, the more he suppressed his anger so he could feel in control, the more he internalized that anger, which inevitably end up controlling his actions.

The more he allowed himself to let go of his need to control every situation, the more he accepted the belief that manhood is not based solely on the power of money, knowledge of sports, or how many women he had conquered. Being a man is about living as a human being first, which includes being supportive, nurturing, loving, and responsible. This realization alone, helped Anthony start the process of real change internally and externally.

Like so many people who develops a controlling behavior pattern as a way to satisfy certain needs, he also recognized how his pattern of manipulations started while growing up with his mother and sister. He was also very much aware of the fact that the illusions of power and control through gaining wealth had not filled the void in his life which he had so tenaciously pursued.

After nearly eight months of counseling, Anthony realized he was not too old to change, find a companion, start a family, and live a relaxed and comfortable life.

Anthony hired a financial corporation to manage his business ventures without his involvement in the day-to-day operations.

Treatment for his swollen prostate was successful. After several dates, Anthony finally made a romantic connection with a 32 year old nurse named Marva, whom he described as charismatic, independent, and a loving woman who makes him feel alive and youthful. He described the type of happiness, joy, and pleasure he had not previously experienced.

The case of the Soubrette family

It was the top of the ninth inning, the score was 7- 4 in favor of the visiting team whose pitcher was recognized as an ace among his teammates. The home team was at bat with the bases loaded and all eyes were on Tom as he ran from the dugout. Tom had already homered in the second inning and had three RBIs in his subsequent visits to the plate. The hometown crowd was cheering wildly, begging for a miracle win, even though their team was trailing by three points with two outs. First pitch, a 95-mph fastball, was a strike.

When the count was full—3 balls, 2 strikes, Tom planted his feet firmly for the final and decisive hit. He swung hard, making contact with the ball just as it was descending. It was a home run!

Thomas "Tom" Jefferson Soubrette, was a popular high school senior and athlete. In addition to being captain of his high school baseball team, he was voted twice as winner of the Most Valuable Boys Athlete Award in his sophomore and junior year. He also excelled in track and field events by winning the 4X400 meter relay and the triple jump contest.

Tom was a good student and a mannerly son. He and his girlfriend, Lucinda "Lucy" Bangs, a junior in high school had been sweethearts since the ages of 14 and 13 respectively. Lucy was also an honor student and quite popular among teachers and students.

Tom and Lucy had promising futures. Tom had been recommended for a college athletic scholarship. There were many who believed he was eligible as a potential draftee for the Pittsburgh Pirates of the National Baseball League.

Lucy was in line for an academic scholarship to attend Duquesne University, located near their hometown in Pittsburgh, Pennsylvania, after graduating from high school. She wanted to major in pediatric medicine, and become a pediatrician.

Due to their moral upbringing, Tom and Lucy were strong enough to say no to the use of drugs and alcohol, but their raging hormones and heavy petting led to several after school quickies (sexual episodes).

At the age of 16, Lucy became pregnant. Tom decided to drop out of his senior year of high school to support Lucy and their baby. He started full time employment at the steel mill where his father had been employed for 21 years.

Tom was the middle child of three offsprings born to Mr. and Mrs. Leroy Soubrette. He had an older brother, and a sister.

Mr. and Mrs. Soubrette, were both of African descent. Mr. Soubrette was a black Creole born in Louisiana. Mrs. Soubrette was an African American born and raised in Pittsburgh. They were hard working honest people who had spent most of their adult lives struggling to earn a decent living so that they could help their three children live an easier life than either of them had while growing up.

Mrs. Soubrette was employed at a factory, manufacturing radio parts. Mr. Soubrette was a high school drop out. He married Tom's mother shortly after she graduated from high school because she was pregnant, which led him to constantly remind his children of the importance of earning a good education and acquiring a marketable skill before marrying and starting a family. The two incomes between Mr. and Mrs. Soubrette, had allowed them to purchase a small single-family, three bedroom, one bathroom house in the Beltzhoover section of Pittsburgh.

Mr. and Mrs. Soubrette had ambitious plans for their three children. Shortly after the birth of their first child Lawrence, they moved out of the one-room apartment into a new single-family house, and started a savings account for Lawrence's college education. They also started a similar savings account following the birth of their second son, Tom, and for their daughter, Stacy. After graduating from high school, Lawrence entered medical school, which made Mr. and Mrs. Soubrette feel extremely proud.

Silently, Lawrence had always been Mrs. Soubrette's favorite child. Perhaps, it was because he was her first child, born when she was only eighteen, and represented the success of her developing skills as a mother. Although, Tom and Stacy had no doubts about her love for them.

Mrs. Soubrette was a kind and generous woman, who treated everyone she met fairly and with respect. It would be difficult to find anyone that did not admire her. No matter what the circumstances were, she always had a calm and pleasant demeanor, which made it easier for others to relate to, and confide in her. Because of her consoling nature, Mr. Soubrette frequently told friends that she keeps him on the "straight and narrow."

Like Lawrence, Tom was also an honor student, but wanted to major in business administration, rather than pursue his parent's choice of medicine or law. The fact that Lawrence was never interested in sports and Tom excelled in sports competition, made Tom, his father's favorite. Of course, both parents insisted that they always treated all of their children the same.

Before marriage and working at the steel mill, Mr. Soubrette was a musician. Once a year, he would travel to the annual Southwest Louisiana Zydeco Festival in Plaisance.

When the children were younger and growing up, usually after paying the mortgage, household bills and groceries, very little if any funds was available for travel or social activities. During the earlier years, Mr. Soubrette was often in a foul mood and complained incessantly about "too many responsibilities and not having any fun in his life."

Much of Tom's participation and achievements in sports were due primarily to his tenacious efforts to please his father and win his approval.

When the news was announced that their 17 year old son, Tom, had dropped out of school to become a father, instead of attending college on an athletic scholarship as had been expected, Mr. Soubrette was heartbroken. This was more than Mr. Soubrette thought he could handle. Believing that his son's life was doomed to repeat a life of hard work and low wages without a proper education or skill. Mr. Soubrette reacted with anger and threatened to throw his son out of his house. He reminded Tom of how hard he and his mother had worked and sacrificed since his birth, so that he could receive a quality education and a better future.

Following two weeks of indulging in anger and self-pity, Mr. Soubrette finally agreed with his wife that Tom was smart and mature enough to take responsibility for his behavior and choices. Mr. Soubrette also agreed with his wife to meet Lucy and her family.

Lucy was the youngest of two daughters. Her mother, Miss Jesse Tolby was a single parent and employed in the same factory as Mrs. Soubrette, although they had never met.

Mr. and Mrs. Soubrette recognized the pregnancy placed a much more severe hardship on Miss Jesse who resided in a two bedroom apartment, also located in the inner city.

Miss Jesse was struggling economically, trying to provide for her two daughters on her low income. She was a proud woman who refused to accept any kind of welfare assistance. She frequently worked overtime to compensate for her low wages, which minimized the amount of time she had to supervise two teenage girls. Her long working hours was also motivated by a desire to help her daughters achieve their dreams for successful careers. She wanted so very much for Lucy to become the first member of her family to attend college.

Miss Jesse and the Soubrettes recognized that Tom and Lucy were in love and were determined to maintain the pregnancy while making plans to marry.

Tom proved to be a hard worker at the steel mill and received several written letters of recognition from his supervisor. He also attended an adult education class two evenings of the week to earn his high school diploma.

Mr. Soubrette felt proud of his son's initiatives. He became convinced that Tom would not be a failure in his life or allow life's adversities to prevent him from achieving his dreams.

At the age of 18, Tom became a father of a healthy baby boy, earned his high school equivalence diploma, and was promoted to a higher salary, almost equal to his dad's.

Tom and Lucy decided to name their son after Tom's father, Leroy Soubrette II. This made Mr. Soubrette feel very proud. It also changed his life. Seldom if ever did he complain about spending money on his family. He was almost always in a cheerful mood, and constantly bragging about his son the supervisor "wearing a white shirt and tie."

As part of his daily routine, Mr. Soubrette was heard telling everyone and anyone in sight, "My grandson can do this, and my grandson could do that."

Since the discovery of their pregnancy, Tom and Lucy abstained from sexual activities. They were still very much in love, but vowed to maintain their commitment to each other without sex until they could afford to marry. They came close to engaging in sexual intercourse on a few occasions, but during each attempt, Tom became overwhelmed with anxiety about the possibility of Lucy becoming pregnant again. Unaware of the real reason he could not perform, Tom blamed his situation on the discomfort of using a condom.

In addition to attending night school to further his education, Tom also became a workaholic, which was his way of proving his masculinity to Lucy and regaining his father's approval.

Lucy also returned to school and completed her high school education. Prior to her pregnancy and becoming a mother, she wanted a job that would allow her to work with children. Due to the parenting skills she acquired while attending two parent education classes, she decided to study early childhood education at a local community college.

Following three years of celibacy, Tom and Lucy's relationship had matured and grown stronger. In the process of learning how to communicate, work and plan together, as well as enjoy each others company while building their careers and providing for their son they became best friends as well as parents.

The responsibilities of parenthood had helped Tom and Lucy mature beyond their chronological age.

Tom at the age of 20, and Lucy at the age of 19, entered the holy bond of matrimony as husband and wife. During their wedding ceremony, they included in their wedding vows "To love one another forever, despite any obstacles they may be confronted with in the future."

As a gift from Tom's parents, they spent two weeks in

Hawaii for their honeymoon. Due to Tom's success on his job, his marital status, and his intense love for Lucy, he did not experience any anxieties or sexual repression while on their honeymoon. After the wedding and honeymoon, Lucy and Lil Leroy moved into the Soubrette's home with Tom.

Although they were young, Tom and Lucy's relationship continued to be strengthened by the strong support they received from their family. Even before the wedding, Miss Jesse and the Soubrettes had developed a close bond and were accepted as extended family members. Since the birth of Lil Leroy, Lucy and Miss Jesse had allowed Mr. and Mrs. Soubrette unlimited access for visitation. After Miss Jesse's oldest daughter graduated from high school, she entered the Peace Corp and traveled abroad. Left alone in her apartment, Miss Jesse would occasionally spend the night, weekend, and several holidays at the Soubrette's home.

Mr. Soubrette convinced Mrs. Soubrette and Miss Jesse on the idea of purchasing a larger house, so that they could all live together as a family. With shared expenses for a huge down payment and a low monthly mortgage, they purchased a 14 room colonial house with five bedrooms, each with its own private bathroom, located in a moderate income neighborhood on a fenced in one and a half-acre property.

After the high school and college graduation of their daughter, Mr. and Mrs. Soubrette were able to pay off all of their debts, purchase luxury items, plan vacations, and supplement their retirements with additional savings. They were far from being identified as wealthy, but had at least achieved the status of feeling debt-free.

After Mrs. Soubrette retired from her factory job. She and Mr. Soubrette tried to convince Miss Jesse to retire, but at 52, she said she was too young to retire.

Miss Jesse no longer had to work over time, and for the first time in her life she was able to purchase needed items for herself without worrying about the cost. She felt very proud of her daughters and excited about their acceptance as members of the Soubrette's family. Shortly after her birth, Miss Jesse was raised by her grandmother until the age of eleven. After her grandmother passed, she lived in foster care until the age of seventeen. She did not have any other family members other than her two daughters. She had often dreamed about having a loving extended family like the Soubrettes and felt empowered by their spiritual relationship.

Miss Jesse's oldest daughter, during her frequent visits home, referred to Mr. and Mrs. Soubrette as her uncle and auntie. Lucy called them "Dad and Big Mama," respectively.

Ironically, Mrs. Soubrette, who grew up with two brothers and no sister, was excited about identifying Miss Jesse, as her sister.

For the first July 4th weekend celebrated in their new home, Lawrence, now a medical doctor, returned home for a visit with his wife and newborn daughter. That weekend celebration was marked as the family's first annual family reunion. Subsequently, each Fourth of July became the most anticipated and celebrated holiday for every member of the Soubrette family.

Lucy completed her two-year college education and obtained a day care license. She convinced Mrs. Soubrette to assist her in managing a pre-school and after-school day care program at the house.

Eventually, the program became so successful they had to hire additional staff and search for another building. They purchased an old abandoned house, had it remodeled to pass code inspections, and licensed as a day care center.

After earning his master's degree in business administration, Tom became a manager at the steel mill, and his salary exceeded his father's.

Mr. Soubrette, finally decided to retire, after 33 years of employment at the mill. He was immediately hired by his daughter-in-law and wife, at the Soubrette's Day Care Center. He was placed in charge of the janitorial and repair services. Feeling a sense of autonomy for the first time in his life, while enjoying his role as a grandfather, he was happier and more content than he had ever thought possible.

It seemed that Lil Leroy had united two families and made them one with love. Tom and Lucy's bond had also helped their parents overcome obstacles and achieve their dreams.

It is simply amazing what can be accomplished with the support of a loving and caring family. Yet despite the lack of continuity in all family relationships, in addition to the numerous rapid sociological changes occurring within our modern day family system.

The concept of a family as an institution continues to serve as a basic unit for meeting many basic human needs. Including the human need which the family has long served—providing for the care and rearing of children. Of course, modern times, however, now dictates needs beyond providing food, clothing, and shelter. The family must continue to function as:

1. A social environment for the affectional bond of family relationships, where children first learn how to love and be loved.

2. An environment where children learn the difference between right and wrong.

3. An environment where children develop a sense of personal identity—emotionally, psychologically, socially, and physically.

Chapter VIII

COPING WITH LIFE CRISES

Among the millions of questions often asked about life, one stands out as wishful thinking for many, but one which inspires hope for everyone—"Is it humanly possible to live a full and healthy life here on earth without encountering one of life's crises?"

I can not count the number of times I have heard someone ask whether it was possible to live his or her life without making a mistake, having a problem, or encountering some type of burden.

Most mistakes are based on poor judgement, lack of knowledge or insufficient information, inattention, or viewed as a simple human error. Especially, if the mistake was not intentional or done out of malice.

When most people find themselves in a difficult situation, which requires an answer, quick solution, or must make an important decision about a particular matter, can either view their situation as a problem that must be confronted, or as a crisis that may change their lives.

A crisis is believed to be a problematic or painful situation, which forces an individual to make a decision about new and unexpected circumstances that occurs in life. Many, view a crisis as an unstable situation in one's financial, health, or social life.

Most adults, are very much aware of the fact that a crisis can occur at any time to anyone. For example, a catastrophic illness to a person without health insurance can lead to financial ruins, in addition to poor or debilitating health. Unemployment, bankruptcy or losing one's life savings are financial situations often viewed as human life crises. Living with a mental illness, confronting a terminal illness, becoming disabled due to loss of limb or other vital body parts are often viewed as health related crises. Loss of a loved one, experiencing the pain of a divorce, losing custody of your children, being evicted from your apartment, or losing your home are all crises which could occur in one's life.

A person struggling with low self-esteem, extreme loneliness, or an inability to get along with others may view their situation as a personality conflict or a crisis. A teenager trying hard to fit in socially with his or her peers may view rejection and ridicule as a crisis.

Ideally, life would be less complicated if everyone had a crystal ball that could predict the future, offer a map of life with an opportunity to ward off disaster, hardships, sickness, and prevent tragedies.

Realistically, for most human beings, life involves a series of struggles from birth to death.

An individual's ability to endure or cope, is when one is able to control his/her behavior and deal effectively with different crises that arise in life.

Coping with any of life's myriad of problems during the stages of human growth and development, makes all human beings realize that life is a condition, which includes a series of struggles between birth and death. A struggle between efforts, choices, decisions, and judgements, which result in triumphs, achievements, and success, or failure and defeat.

In many families, after a child is born, family members usually get excited when the child first open his or her eyes and make contacts of recognition with parents. Everyone gets excited when the child starts crawling, walking, talking, and eating independently. Completing toilet training is almost always considered an acknowledged victory.

As a child grows, he/she is expected to learn his/her ABC's, spell, write name, and learn something about the ways of the world. Between daycare, kindergarten, and grade school, they must spend, at least, the next 14 years of their lives in an institution of learning. Just think how excited everyone is during high school graduation.

After graduating from high school, decisions must be made about preparing for adulthood—whether to work, attend college, enter the military, or travel around the world.

Between the ages of 18 and 21, if you are unable to decide the direction or path that you would like to take in preparing for your future, you are considered to be at a "crossroad" in your life, and based on your emotional response or the reaction of your family members, this situation could be viewed as a serious crisis. The choices you make will determine how you plan to live your life, and whether you will resolve or prolong your crisis.

During another stage of life, mostly between the ages of 41 and 62 (plus or minus a couple of years), when most men start viewing themselves as getting old, or as simply "old." They usually experience what has become known as a "midlife crisis." For some men, this becomes a turning point in their lives, when they suddenly feels the urge to identify with the younger generations.They change their usual style of dressing. The conservative suits and ties they once believed made them look distinguish, no longer fits their new image. Now baggy pants pulled down midstream with the shirt on the outside becomes much more comfortable.

A few wives with husbands in their 50s, 60s, and some 70s complained about their husband's new interest in watching hip hop music on television, and taking them to night clubs where only "teenyboppers" hangout."

There were also a few, very few, complaints about the

husbands who used viagra or some other drug which made their husbands act like they had found the magic cure for old age or his version of the fountain of youth.

There are numerous "wives' tales" about husbands who quit their jobs, divorced their wives for younger women, and spent their retirement savings on a new car, boat, motorcycle, and another house they considered more appropriate for their new lifestyle.

Surprisingly, some researchers have indicated that most men experiencing midlife crisis are not aware that there is anything wrong with their behavior other than a feeling of urgency to race against time while some of the most important physiological and psychological aspects of their manhood are deteriorating.

Both male and female midlife crises have been the cause of numerous hardships in relationships, especially the breakup of families. As well as the cause of many men and women to suffer an emotional breakdown.

Women also experience a turning point in their lives, better known as the menopause stage—a natural biological process in the human growth and development of females. For many women, menopause starts in their 30s, 40s, 50s, or 60s. It is a stage of a woman's life when she stops having menstrual periods. The average age for most women is after 50 when their estrogen and progesterone hormones produce less than what is required to maintain regular monthly periods. Like the male midlife crisis, not all women experience menopause the same way. Some view their menopausal stage as a crisis. Especially those who are confronted with the possibility of developing a life threatening physical illness or complication. As well as those who have difficulty managing some of the painful physical and emotional symptoms, like bloating, headaches, fatigue, depression, loss of sexual desire, and other stressful symptoms.

As humans continue to grow older, some situations, which are often viewed as crises are just a natural part of life. Such as many of the unexpected circumstances that are caused by sickness, aging, and death.

Of course, not all illnesses and diseases are part of the normal process of aging, although many are associated with "old age." For example, research studies have shown that Alzheimer's disease occurs mostly in people over the age of 85, even though there are several reported cases of people who are much younger suffering with the disease. Coping with the relationship changes that accompany Alzheimer's disease can be a crisis for a spouse or family member.

There are literally thousands of families taking care of a parent, spouse, or another family member who have been incapacitated by injury, illness, or disease. Some were disabled after a fall, automobile accident, or stroke, and some were due to parkinson's disease—a progressive nervous condition, characterized by muscular tremor and partial paralysis.

Different people have different ways of coping or managing new and unexpected changes, stress, and conflicts in their lives. Research studies have shown that an individual's ability to cope with adversity is developed early in childhood.

As a social worker at Family and Children's Services, I received training for intensive and supportive family therapy. Part of my clinical training with other staff members, included observing children's behavior behind a one way mirror while they played in the agency's play therapy room. By observing their social interactions, one could readily observe how some of the children handled stress, failure, aggression, and solved problems.

In 1988, my wife and I hosted a birthday party in our backyard for a family member. While video taping, I watched our eleven months old niece trying to walk independently. She managed to take a few steps before falling, but immediately pulled herself up and tried again. Later, I observed her trying to step off the paved driveway onto the lawn, which was about a four or five inch decline. With one foot on the driveway, and the other foot on the lawn, she fell, again. I started to lift her up, but decided to continue video taping, to see how she would solve her dilemma. She pulled herself up and tried it again.

Rather than just walking on the paved driveway, she appeared determined to conquer the task of stepping off the driveway onto the lawn. After falling down, again and again, and pulling herself up, she was not crying, nor appeared to be injured, but had a very determined look on her face, and an obvious will to accomplish her goal.

After gaining her composure, she stood, looked at the driveway beneath her feet and down at the lawn before attempting to step on the lawn again. On her next try, she succeeded by stepping off the driveway onto the lawn without falling. I led everyone watching in a big cheer to acknowledge her success. Her mother and father had been watching anxiously, and seemingly worried that her falling might cause an injury. I told them that their daughter had just solved a major problem in her life, which could reflect her attitude about future problems. I also announced that she would grow up to become a bold and courageous child. About 14 years later, my wife and I went to see our niece play in a community basketball game. The girl's team played against the boy's community basketball team. The girl's team won. In high school, she was a star basketball player and an honor student.

In 2005 she graduated from high school with a sports award and scholarship for "outstanding attitudes and demonstrated good sportsmanship." As of this very writing, she is a freshman in college. Her efforts reminded me that it is always up to the individual to decide, whether to get up after falling down, or give up and stay down. Whether to accept what appears to be an impossible challenge or accept defeat by not trying.

Of course, I realize that confronting a life crisis, such as recovering from a life-threatening illness or injury, and overcoming a depression due to the death of a loved one are far from being a fair comparison. My focus, however, was on how children start learning how to cope with disappointment and failure.

I believe that if one learns how to confront and resolve the challenge of new and unexpected circumstances, as well as adversity early in life, they will be better prepared to cope with different crises later in life.

The ability to cope also refers to an individual striving for a successful conclusion or end to a problem, and the positive adjustment one makes in his or her life, regardless of age.

I know there are many who find it extremely difficult to cope with the negative circumstances surrounding their lives, however, they need to be encouraged to continue seeking a solution. A crisis can be a turning point, which could result in a negative change for the worst or a chance for improvement, and a change for the better.

Mrs. Zypries

A 61 year-old woman with cancer was frightened, emotionally upset, and angry about her recent diagnosis. She had an obsession about collecting all kinds of stuff and storing it in her house. She had never used some of the items nor had any intentions of using.

After several years of neglect and numerous complaints from neighbors, the landlord finally visited Mrs. Zypries' house to make repairs, but was unable to enter due to the clutter.

There were many new items just stored or stacked in an empty bedroom until she ran out of space. Then she started storing items in the next room, and when that room became too cluttered, she stacked items in her kitchen, living room, and bedroom.

So much clutter existed in her home she could barely move about or use her furniture and other facilities. She slept on her sofa, which she also shared with stacks of outdated newspapers, magazines, and other debris.

Based on the amount of clutter she had collected and stored, Mrs. Zypries' behavior appeared to be what some people refer to as "pack rats" and some psychologists call "hoarding behavior." It is believed that hoarding behavior is one of the symptoms of obsessive-compulsive disorder (OCD).

Mrs. Zypries' compulsive hoarding behavior started at the age of 47 after her left leg was amputated due to diabetes. She was living alone without any family ties or social support, which made it easier for her to conceal her behavior. The most frequent visitor was the mail carrier who delivered the packages to her front door. She spent endless hours watching television and ordering items from the home shopping network.

Amazingly, she did not think it was a problem to have all that stuff in and around her house. She simply justified her actions by saying, "I don't throw nothing away that I might need later on." The problem was, she did not need or use any of the collected items stored in her house or yard.

In addition to the fear of being evicted from her rented house, the landlord had doubled her monthly rent and refused to make needed repairs or improvements that would bring the house into compliance with the local housing code until she got rid of the clutter or vacate the premises.

The on-going conflict with her landlord added to her existing depression. She refused to leave her home and would not follow up with her scheduled medical appointments.

Arrangements had to be made for her to be placed in an assisted-care facility. She objected to the placement, saying that she was ready to die and if she had a chance to live again, she would refuse the opportunity.

During an interview, she described her life as one constant battle of "ups-and-downs." She was born on a farm under extreme impoverished conditions, which caused her to start working at an early age. She was only allowed to attend school until she learned how to read and write. Her parents were share croppers who were too tired and busy to have any time for nurturing her or her siblings. She married at a young age in an attempt to escape poverty. She had been married three times and given birth to two children, following three miscarriages. Her first husband was killed in combat during World War II. She described her second husband as abusive, unfaithful, and unemployed. He was killed in a fight over a gambling debt. Her third husband was described as the only man she ever loved. He died of a stroke, and she had been suffering with a broken heart ever since his death. Both of her two children were dead. Her daughter died from an overdose of drugs at the age of 23, and her 17 year-old son was killed in a gang related drive-by-shooting.

From Mrs. Zypries' point of view, the intermittent pleasure and joy she had experienced in her life were overshadowed by persistent hardships and misery. At that stage of her life she had made a personal decision to give up and stop trying to cope.

Before having Mrs. Zypries admitted into the hospital, she had to make a decision about removing her collected items so it would not be a shock to her when she returned. The situation was carefully discussed, including how she would be able to move about her house freely, use her furniture, bathroom, and kitchen facilities. It took several days of negotiating until she agreed to accept a neighbor's offer to coordinate a tag sale in her front yard.

Mrs. Zypries pointed out the items she wanted to sale, or keep, and agreed to donate her other "treasures" to Salvation Army and Good Will Industries.

Following numerous interviews, arranging transportation for medical appointments, and resolving the dispute with her landlord, she was able to return to her home with regular home care supervision.

In the midst of the positive changes, Mrs Zypries developed a renewed commitment to life and living. She also received the necessary prosthetics, which enabled her to walk independently again. She confided that no one had ever helped her to that extent. She also agreed to accept daily transportation to a senior center for a hot meal, socialization, and entertainment. My last interview with her revealed that staff members at the center were requesting her assistance with the care of other members, which helped her feel needed, and restored her passion for living.

Most people, experience some type of crisis in his or her life, or a period of transition, which can initiate a life-review process and an assessment of where one stands with respect to their age and progression in life. After all, it is considered "normal" for human beings to experience various changes in their life.

Of course, many abrupt changes often produce stress, which results in a temporary disruption in one's life. Research indicates that there is no "typical response" as to how every one will react to any given crisis. A large number of studies reflect a wide variation on how most people respond to tragedy. Some people recover quickly from their loss, or at least learn to live with their adversity. Others, just seem to progress through different changes while attempting to cope.

A temporary problem or disruption in one's life following a crisis such as the death of a loved one, when people are more susceptible to stress and anxiety, short-term counseling or brief psychotherapy known as crisis intervention may be all that is required for assistance. In many cases, some individuals chose new paths or careers as their means of coping or moving on with their lives.

After an unmarried mother lost her only child in a hit-and-run, drunk driving automobile accident, she decided to join "Mother's Against Drunk Driving (MADD)" as a way of coping with her grief. Her participation led to a new career in creating effective legislation that helped protect others from similar tragedies.

A man who lost his loving wife to leukemia went through several stages of grief, anxiety, anger, and depression before he joined a local organization to help raise awareness and funds for advance research. He discovered that his new found talents as a public speaker and fund raiser was far more effective and fulfilling than his 19 year career as a carpenter.

There have also been studies conducted, indicating that some people never recover from their trauma. I have read numerous clinical cases about people who continued feeling depressed and anxious for several months or years after surviving a traumatic event such as war, rape, kidnapping, being burnt in a fire, near-drowning, or other near-death experiences. Including survivors who were forced to standby helplessly while witnessing the loss of a loved one in a fire, drowning, an automobile accident, or other fatalities.

As a former coordinator of the outpatient treatment

clinic for the Regional Narcotics Program (RNP), during the mid-seventies, I observed many clients struggling with various crises. For many, the use of alcohol and drugs had become their way of trying to cope.

It was at RNP where I provided counseling and referral services for several clients struggling with symptoms known as a Posttraumatic Stress Disorder (PTSD)—A term used in psychiatry to describe an emotional reaction developed after experiencing or witnessing a life-threatening, or traumatic event.

I interviewed several Vietnam veterans who had survived military combat. Many of whom, had initially found it difficult to adjust from society's standards and expectations of non-violence and aggression, to learning how to become killers.

I also interviewed clients who had suffered repeated physical and emotional abuse as children, or had witnessed abuse, or a serious accident which in some cases resulted in the loss of a life, or lives.

A traumatic event can cause one to respond with fear, terror, numbness, helplessness, depression, or several other anxiety related disorders. Individuals suffering with PTSD often complained about recurring and distressing memories of the painful event. Some of my clients described how their inability to stop remembering led to difficulty sleeping, concentrating, use of drugs, and other self-destructive behavior.

During the seventies and eighties, I was acquainted with several Vietnam veterans who had returned home after engaging in military combat. Some of them offered chilling details of their experiences. Most were able to make the necessary adjustments back into society by connecting with family, friends, and gain productive employment. Yet there were many that returned home emotionally wounded and suffering with PTSD.

One of the veterans interviewed, described his child-hood years as peaceful and fun-filled, and his relationship with his parents as "ideal." He never had a fight or violent dispute with anyone before his military experience in Vietnam. He was drafted into the military at the age of 18, and was one of the first American combat troops to land in Da Nang, Vietnam in 1965. During his time in Vietnam, he witnessed the death of numerous men, women, and children.

One of his recurring nightmares involved vivid images of the war, and the imploding of a Vietnamese man's body from a bomb.

After serving his time in Vietnam, he returned home, moved in with his parents, but were unable to relate to them. He found it extremely difficult to adjust to the home and middle-class neighborhood he had grown up in. His neighbors and old friends viewed him as peculiar, espe-cially when he would be seen wearing his military uniform, walking up and down the streets talking to himself. Repeated arguments with his father about his refusal to search for employment led to his moving out of the house and living on the street, homeless, and unemployed. He was frequently arrested for possession of drugs, criminal activities and other anti-social behavior. During one of his arrests, the judge gave him the option of entering a resi-dential drug treatment program or serving six months in jail. He chose jail. Shortly after completing his sentence, he was arrested again for possession of narcotics and sent to RNP for evaluation and treatment. Part of his assessment revealed that he had symptoms of a Posttraumatic Stress Disorder. One of the counselors in the residential treatment program requested me to talk to him. I was able to convince him to seek therapy in a long-term residential drug treatment facility rather than contin-ue his on-going behavior and arrests. After completing the detoxification program, he served 18 months in a residential program, which included individual and group psychotherapy.

Before being released, part of his rehabilitation involved serving as a peer counselor to other residents in the program. He was so effective that he was hired as a full time drug treatment counselor.

Another veteran returned home from Vietnam, physically wounded. He was confined to a wheelchair, paralyzed from the waist down, but was determined not to feel defeated or be viewed as a victim. He was well aware of the fact that his wounds had dealt him a difficult hand, which he had to play in order to cope with the new set of circumstances that had been thrust upon his life.

Prior to his entering the military, he was active in sports. He had assumed several leadership responsibilities in his school, community, and at home. Starting at an early age, his parents taught him how to take responsibility for his actions and decisions. When he was 16-years-old, he broke his arm and had his shoulder dislocated while playing football. One year after surgery, he wanted to play both football and basketball in his senior year of high school. After his doctor signed a medical release, his parents allowed him to use his own judgement, since he would be the one to live with the consequences of his decision. So when he returned home from Vietnam, he decided to participate in the wheelchair athletics program. He also participated in numerous sport events for various charities in his community.

Although his major source of income was from the military as a disabled veteran, he chose to seek employment and live independently. His enthusiastic spirit and will to live his life to his fullest potential allowed him to find effective ways of coping and living a fulfilling life. He was recognized as a role model and a hero.

During the 60s and 70s, community mental health centers, crisis intervention services, and halfway houses were established in an effort to assist people who were having different types of crises. Some of the services offered, included outpatient clinics for emergency assistance and a crisis hotline where people could telephone and receive immediate counseling, information, or referrals for additional treatment.

Increasingly, in the new millennium, many individuals are seeking psychological counseling to enable them to cope with their lives amid the rapid changes in our modern society. People should be encouraged to continue seeking help for a crisis that is perceived as overwhelming. There are many that do not seek treatment, as a result, what might have been just a temporary crisis often turn into a mental or physical illness.

Of course, we all know how easy it is to say that one should pick themselves up and move on with their lives, but if you have ever experienced a painful loss, or a traumatic event, then you probably also know how difficult it can be to recover.

The key to coping with a life crisis, is to continue seeking an effective solution to the problem.

Throughout history, human beings have always found a way to overcome various life crises, and if the human species are to continue, we must all find ways to overcome our struggles and fight for survival, despite our differences.

Learning how to cope with adversity is about developing survival skills and problem solving techniques that will enable you to maintain a sense of emotional balance and stability.

Attention Deficit Disorder

It appears that the ages of young people being incarcerated are becoming younger and younger with each passing day.

Televisions, radios, and newspapers are often inundated with reports of young people committing criminal acts of violence. Many young children are being charged as adults for crimes that they are unable to describe or explain.

Our courts, juvenile detention centers, jails and prisons are becoming over crowded with children who have not reached the age of adolescence.

Increasingly, we are discovering that many of these young people could have been spared from incarceration. The lives of their victims could also have been saved, if a proper diagnosis had been made, and the proper treatment administered during the earlier signs of mental disorders.

It has been estimated that over 20 million men, women, and children residing in the United States suffer from Attention Deficit/ Hyperactivity Disorder (ADHD). Studies show that there are millions of other people with ADHD type characteristics, but are not reported because they were not properly diagnosed.

Several studies have revealed that parents of children with ADHD, most often have some of the ADHD traits, but were never properly diagnosed as children, therefore they grew up struggling with attention related problems themselves or were diagnosed as "hyperactive" and were told that their symptoms would disappear as they grow older.

According to available researched information, the exact causes of ADHD, formerly known as ADD, remains unknown.

Some researchers suggest that the disorder is brain based and is genetically transmitted from a parent or grand parent to a child. Some researchers have claimed that scientific evidence strongly suggests that ADHD is neurologically based. Caused by certain chemicals in the brain's neurotransmitter systems. Neurotransmitters are chemicals which regulate brain cell function. Thus, these chemicals help the brain regulate behavior by sending messages from the brain to different nerve cells and muscles within the body..

Most experts agree that ADHD symptoms often arise in early childhood. It is marked by behaviors that are long lasting and evident for at least six months before the age of seven. A pattern of ADHD symptoms, most often comes to the attention of the parents when the child begins school, due to his/her difficulty in sitting still and concentrating in a classroom setting among other children where there can be a great deal of stimulation.

As a social worker, I had the experience of learning just how much Attention Deficit Disorder and other forms of mental illnesses contributed to the growing deterioration of our young people and their increasing involvement with drugs, crime, violence, and death.

In the 1980's when I started my research on ADD, it was described by different types of behaviors, primarily having to do with hyperactivity, which involves restless or excessive activity. I learned that ADD was not a new illness or condition. Many of the scientists during the earlier years referred to ADD by several different names.

On October 24,1991, I attended a lecture on "Attention Deficit Disorder and Its Effect on Behavior," at Courtland Gardens in Stamford, Connecticut. The lecture was presented by Dr. John J. Ratey, M.D., who was an assistant professor of psychiatry at Harvard Medical School.

Dr. Ratey talked about his extensive research on the neuropsychiatry of developmental disabilities, and the treatment of "aggressive and compulsive behavior in adolescents." During a slide presentation, it was indicated that symptoms of ADD was written about as early as 1845, by Heinrich Hoffman, a German physician and author who wrote short stories, poems, and books on medicine and psychiatry.

During the 1960's, symptoms of the disorder became known as "Minimal Brain Dysfunction" or "MBD." In the 70's, children diagnosed with symptoms of MBD came to be called "hyperactive or hyperkinetic." Many researchers believed, however, that the hyperactivity dissipated around the age of adolescence, and that the problem no longer existed. By 1980, inattention appeared as the primary problem, however, further study revealed that not all children with attention related problems were hyperactive.

Researchers divided the disorder into three subgroups, which reflected ADD individuals with hyperactivity, without hyperactivity, and a third category defined as "Residual Type" referring to individuals with ADD who carried the symptoms into adulthood.

In 1987, the name changed again to reflect the widely held opinion of many researchers that inattention, impulsivity, and hyperactivity were all central characteristics of the disorder. In the Diagnostic and Statistical Manual of Mental Disorders (DSM), published by the American Psychiatric Association, the disorder became known as Attention-deficit Hyperactivity Disorder (ADHD) and a single list of 14 criteria containing features of inattention, impulsivity, and hyperactivity were used to make the diagnosis.

In 1994 the American Psychiatric Association published the fourth edition of the DSM. In this edition, ADHD remained unchanged from the previous 1987 DSM-III

Revised edition. The only difference was the way the name was written, Attention-Deficit/Hyperactivity Disorder. The slash within the label indicated that a person could have primary symptoms of attention-deficit, or hyperactivity disorder, or a combination of inattention and hyperactivity disorder.

The DSM is used by medical and mental health professionals to identify child, adolescent and adult psychiatric, learning, and emotional disorders.

Currently, three types of behaviors are identified in DSM-IV, which might be present when an individual has AD/HD—hyperactivity/impulsivity, distractibility, and inattention. Studies have shown that a person could have one, two, or all three disorders at the same time.

The hyperactivity, in children with ADD, is often recognized by a child running about or climbing on things constantly, difficulty sitting still, fidgeting, tossing and turning during sleep, and always active, as if they have more energy than other children the same age.

The impulsivity, aspect of children with ADD, is most often recognized by a child acting before thinking, shifting quickly from one activity to another, having difficulty organizing schoolwork, frequently calling out in class, and having difficulty waiting a turn in games or group activities.

Distractibility is a problem with children who have problems following instructions because they are easily distracted. In some instances, the child can pay attention for a short period and do quite well in a one-to-one setting. As a result, there appears to be no problem with the child. Quite often, this is rather confusing to many parents who are unable to understand how their child can behave one way at home and yet receive so many complaints about their behavior at school. One of my roles, as a counselor, has been to explain to parents, and some teachers, that it is in a large group setting with increased stimulation that most children with ADHD will have difficulty controlling his/her behavior.

In addition to being easily distracted in a public environment, or large group setting, a child with ADHD, also has difficulty concentrating on schoolwork or focusing other tasks which require sustained attention.They have been known to have problems organizing their activities, remembering where they put things, keeping up with class assignments, and following instructions.

Numerous studies have indicated that children with ADHD who are not properly diagnosed or treated, gradually start feeling frustrated, "turned off" to school, and stop striving for academic achievement. Many find themselves getting into trouble and believing that they are unable to do anything to please others. Eventually, they rebel against established rules and expectations, which often lead to self-destructive behavior or criminal activities.

Some people, frequently describe inattentive children with ADD who are not hyperactive, as slow thinkers, retarded, a "backward child," or the absent-minded professor types. Some of the children in this category, are often confused by their lack of ability to focus on complicated data or complex information and details. I have known some who were afraid to try using a computer, believing it was much too difficult for them to comprehend.

Because children with ADD without hyperactivity, are not constantly jumping up and down or climbing the walls, their inability to focus often does not appear to be a problem until the consistent demand for attention and concentration is required in school, or their parents receive a report card with poor grades.

Despite the large amount of information known about ADHD many children go undiagnosed and their behavior are often misunderstood.

In 2003, during one of my visits to a printing supply company, one of the owners inquired about the article I wrote in Onyx Magazine (2001), on Attention Deficit Disorder(ADD). In the article, I described ADD as a syndrome that has been called one of the most common learning and behavioral problems affecting children in modern society.

The owner wanted to know what a syndrome was, so I described a syndrome as a group of signs and symptoms that collectively characterizes a disease, psychological disorder, or other abnormal conditions. Recognizing the fact that many people find it difficult to relate to a mental or psychological condition and terminology, I used an example of a physical condition to explain a syndrome as a collection of symptoms.

Most people know that a cold is a viral infection of the mucous membranes. I described coughing, sneezing, chills, and a fever as symptoms or characteristics of a cold. Similar to hyperactivity, impulsivity, distractibility and inattention are symptoms of ADHD. Adding that a proper medical examination could determine whether the viral infection is chronic or acute, or if it is a common cold, flu, bronchitis, or pneumonia. Likewise, a thorough examination of people exhibiting symptoms of ADHD is required for a proper diagnosis and treatment.

After I described what a syndrome was, and he said that he understood. He asked if I really believed that some children actually indulge in criminal behavior because of an attention related problem. I explained that not all children with ADHD engage in criminal behavior. Then, he asked, "How is it possible that during the old days, parents raised their children without all of this psycho-babble?" I was told how he and his ten brothers and sisters were raised by parents who believed, "If you spare the rod, you spoil the child." And none of his brothers or sisters had ever been arrested or used drugs.

As he continued talking, he described problems with one of his four children. He said that a teacher told him that his son has "this ADD thing," and he disagreed with the teacher, because neither he nor his wife has any problem with their son at home.

He said, the teacher "accused" his son of not being able to sit still, listen, or pay attention. That he was easily distracted, very forgetful, and always bothering other students in class. He said, "I know the teacher was not describing my son, because he knows what he would get if he did anything like that." I asked him, what would his son get if he discovered that the teacher's description was correct. He immediately said, "A whipping."

I asked if he or his wife had considered having their son examined by a physician, neurologist, or psychologist. He said, "No," because he was certain that nothing was wrong with his son.

About five weeks later, I returned to the same store for printing supplies. I noticed that the owner who quizzed me about ADD during my last visit was not in the shop. One of the other employees said that he was out for a week on a family leave. I later learned that his nine-year old son had attacked his six-year-old daughter.

His situation reminded me of the the fact that most parents viewed raising children as a natural process. Likewise, most parents continue to raised their children similar to the way they had been reared. Even in our modern day society, many parents still do not take the time to read books about child-rearing, or syndromes characterizing mental disorders that affect children, or take modern parenting methods more seriously.

It has always appeared easier for many to relate to a physical disability or handicap than to recognize or try to understand someone with a mental disorder, or a syndrome of mental illness.

If a child was born with a health problem or physical defect, most would not hesitate to seek medical attention. However, thousands of children have been born with some type of mental defect that was not visible or immediately observable, beyond their obvious behavioral problems, but were expected to "grow out of it," without proper treatment.

There are numerous children born with conditions that cause behavioral problems, who are expected to conform to the rules and expectations of society, without proper treatment. Many studies have reported that too many children born with mental defects have been punished if they do not conform to his/her expectations, or have been mistakenly labeled as a "behavior problem child, unmotivated, a trouble maker, or a bad person with an attitude problem."

I have witnessed quite a few situations where a parent spanked an infant or toddler in public for "misbehaving." I have seen this in grocery stores, parks, restaurants, and once in the waiting room of my office building. It was a situation involving a three and a half-year-old child who was born three months prematurely. The trauma of his birth resulted in neurological damage and was believed to be the primary cause of his hyperactive behavior. While the mother was waiting impatiently to see her assigned therapist, she consistently hit the child for not sitting still as was demanded of him, until the receptionist intervened by trying to entertain the child in a calm and cheerful voice.

During the "old days" children born with ADHD, or other neurological or mental disorders were less likely to be examined by a doctor, psychologist, or social worker. Unless their parents were educated, wealthy, or had access to resources. Otherwise, the parents that believed, "If you spare the rod, you spoil the child," would use the rod as a cure for whatever the parent thought was wrong with the child.

Even in school, many of the children born with ADHD were often labeled "learning disabled" or considered to be incorrigible. Many were placed in "special education" or transferred to an alternative educational program that did not address the child's mental disorders.

As a family counselor, my role was to help children and adults with ADHD understand that their emotional, educational, and vocational difficulties may be related to a disability, rather than to some personal failure.

In the seventies, laws were passed, which declared physical punishment as "child abuse." Increasingly, we witnessed numerous groups formed to educate parents and teachers about alternative disciplinary strategies. These efforts led to further studies about the importance of a proper diagnosis and treatment of childhood mental illnesses.

In the 1980s there continued to exist much controversy about the growing number of young people committing crimes with guns, increasing drug addiction, car theft, and gang wars.

In the 1990s, we witnessed 11, 12, and 13 year-old children being arrested for various crimes, many were seen on our television screens smiling and appearing unaware of the seriousness of their situation, or the consequences of their actions.

In 2000 and 2001, we continued witnessing children committing violent crimes with guns, going into schools, killing other students and teachers. We have also witnessed an increased in teenage suicides.

Much of the controversy surrounding children and crime concluded that many of these young people suffered from Attention Deficit/Hyperactivity Disorder, depression, or some other type of mental disorder.

It is vitally important that all children with mental health problems be properly examined, diagnosed and treated before they develop self-destructive behavior, drop out of school, commit a crime, or cause another family to lose a loved one.

Most experts agree that ADHD is a treatable disorder. Numerous studies indicate that children who receive adequate treatment for ADHD have fewer problems with schools, peers, and criminal behavior.

Without a comprehensive evaluation and treatment during the early signs of mental problems, a child could grow into adulthood with serious emotional and social difficulties, which could affect their relationship at work, in a marriage, as a parent, and other circumstances.

Parents, teachers, mental health professionals, or anyone concerned about AD/HD can obtain additional information from the following:

Center for Mental Health Services (CMHS)
P.O. Box 42490
Washington, DC 2001
1-800-789-CMHS

Children and Adults with Attention Deficit Disorders
    (CHADD).
8181 Professional Place (Suite 201)
Landover, MD, 20785
1-800-233-4050

The National Information Center for Children and
    Youth with:
Disabilities (NICHCY)
P.O. Box 1492
Washington, DC 20013

The National Mental Health Association
1-800-969-6642

National Suicide Hotline
1- 800- 784-2433

For emergency medical services, please dial 911 or contact the emergency room of your local hospital.

Depression

As an undergraduate college student in 1964, I did not have any means of transportation and had to walk several miles per day to maintain a part-time job. On my way to work, I walked past a man standing on the street corner, wearing what appeared to be several layers of clothing and a couple of overcoats, talking to himself. He appeared to be wearing the same old clothing whether it was summer or winter. I did not know anything about him, but frequently heard other people refer to him as "Crazy Toetopper."

Each day I walked passed him, I wondered if he had a family or anyone who cared about him, and if he did, why would they allow him to stand on that street corner.

Practically everyday, Mr. Toetopper would be seen walking back and forth with a high level of energy on the same street corner, talking or singing loudly, waving at cars, and greeting people as they walked down the street. Most people would walk in the street to avoid walking directly pass him. Occasionally, a few children would be seen taunting him, until they heard an adult shout their opposition to "Leave Crazy Toetopper along."

Prior to taking an introduction to psychology course in 1964, I knew very little about the dynamics of mental illness, nor do I recall if I had ever heard anyone talk about depression or schizophrenia.

In addition to my undergraduate and graduate college courses, as years passed, I became increasingly interested in reading and learning more about human behavior and why we do the things we do.

As a marriage and family counselor in 1972, I attended an abortion counseling seminar in White Plains, New York, which focused on depression, post-partum psychosis, and other traumatic symptoms encountered by many women after giving birth.

Most people experience some type of melancholy and loneliness, temporarily or for a brief period, but a depression is a form of mental illness in which a person experiences intense sadness and diminished interest in almost all social and work related activities, including activities that they once expressed deep interest.

Depression as an illness may vary in length of time and intensity. A major depression is more intense, prolonged (usually lasts longer than two weeks), and can impair a person's ability to function at work, school, or in most social and marital situations.

Depending on the level of intensity, a major depression is frequently labeled as a manic depressive disorder or bipolar, characterized by severe mood swings ranging between feeling highly excited or energetic, or deep feelings of sadness with little or no energy.

The exact cause of depression is still a debatable issue with tons of published information about cause and effect. The death of a love one appears to produce the most severe and long-lasting distress, although many researchers believe the loss of a love one is not always the cause of a depression or mania.

There are numerous case studies of people who encountered a depression without an obvious reason. In some cases, very talented, successful, and famous men, women, and children have experienced feelings of failure, worthlessness, helplessness, shame, or guilt. Many have also attempted suicide.

It is widely believed that most men are far less likely than women to recognize the symptoms of depression or talk about their feelings. Therefore, according to most statistics, women suffer from depression at a much higher rate than men, and are more likely to be diagnosed and receive treatment.

Some men also view depression and other mood disorders as a "woman's disease." Therefore, some men try to mask their own feelings of sadness, emotional pain, or thoughts of suicide with denial, hard work, alcoholism, or drugs. Several studies have indicated that domestic violence most often involves men and women who were experiencing some form of depression or anxiety disorders, and had not learned how to communicate their feelings and emotions effectively in constructive ways.

Of course, there are certain types of depression which only women experience. Such as:

Premenstrual syndrome (PMS), which many women experience before or during their menstruation. Quite often symptoms includes feeling bloated, irritable, and moodiness.

Post partum depression, which many women experience after giving birth. Common symptoms include, sadness or "baby blues", excessive crying for no apparent reason, change in appetite, insomnia, anxiety, or mood swings. In some cases panic attacks, and suicidal thoughts.

Post partum psychosis, which usually results in perceiving danger when there is no danger, experienced by some women after having an abortion or giving birth. A woman with post partum psychosis most often display similar symptoms of post partum depression, but will also experience a break with reality. She might appear paranoid and present symptoms of delusions, hallucinations, anger, and hostility. Frequently, her suspicion and distrust involves close family members, a husband, or child.

Most women who experience post partum psychosis will do so shortly after giving birth or having an abortion. For married women, this critical time has led to high rates of divorce. During this critical stage of post partum psychosis some women accuse their husbands of infidelity or abuse, and in some cases, view their child or children as being possessed by demons. One woman described how she experienced a panic attack and attempted suicide for three consecutive years. Each episode occurred on or near the date of her aborted fetus' predicted birthdate.

There are studies reporting that intense sadness and severe mood swings are due to a chemical or hormonal imbalance in the brain, which affects one's thoughts, emotions, behavior, and body.

Postpartum depression, which literally means "depression following childbirth" is believed to be caused by the loss or lowering of hormones. It has been observed that during a woman's pre-menstrual, menstruation, and/or pregnancy, her hormones fluctuates between high and low hormonal levels, which can trigger emotional stress or a depression.

It has also been observed that following childbirth and adapting to a new baby, many women have been treated for postpartum depression after complaining about experiencing psychotic symptoms such as delusions and hallucinations.

Men, as well as women, should become more informed about depression as a human mood disorder that can occur to anyone at anytime and learn that it is a treatable illness.

Everyone needs to know that experiencing a depression is not a sign of weakness or effeminacy. It just proves that you are human.

Since 1972, I have counseled both men and women during family, marriage, or individual counseling sessions who described various symptoms of depression.

The following quote is an excerpt from one of my 1976 lectures on depression:

"Last month, you celebrated your fiftieth birthday. You were complimented for your great looks and youthful appearance, following 27 years of marriage to your high school sweetheart, and three healthy children. You were successful in your career and were contemplating retirement at the age of 55. You were "living large."

Suddenly, the company where you have been employed for 23 years announced plans for restructuring, and started downsizing. Your department was the first to close.

For the first time in your life, since high school, you are out of a job, and are unable to locate another job with similar responsibilities and income. You are forced to start training for a new career at an entry-level position.

After completing your new career training classes, you are unable to find employment. Your workmen's compensation has ended and your mortgage payments are in arrears.

One day, while lying on the couch watching television, one of your numerous favorite programs is interrupted for a "Breaking news" announcement of a school bus accident. You later learn that your youngest child, age 17, was killed in that bus accident while returning from a soccer game.

You and your spouse start arguing more frequently and bitterly. Eventually, the tension and unresolved conflicts leads to a mutual agreement for a legal separation.

Living alone, you separate yourself from your family and friends. You stop participating in your usual social activities. You find yourself sleeping longer hours, sometimes as much as 16 hours a day, and when awaken, you feel tired and drained of energy. You no longer have an appetite, and have difficulty thinking and making plans for your future. You feel worthless and simply can not think of anything positive about your life. You define yourself as a failure and become convinced that you are a hopeless case. Increasingly, you feel ashamed and guilty—which lead to thinking about death and suicide."

The above quote was used to describe how easy a man or woman could encounter a depression.

Several case studies indicate that some people are more susceptible to the emotional pain of depression than others. When some people become overwhelmed or overloaded with stress, they have the tendency to easily become depressed due to what some researchers have identified as an "inherited trait or predisposition." In such cases, an individual's attitude can often be influenced by his or her depressed feelings, which distorts their sense of reality and lead to feelings of hopelessness, rather than recognize the positive aspects occurring in his or her life. For example, a person encountering a conflict, which under most circumstances would be considered a small matter requiring a simple solution by making a decision, may feel overwhelmed and become depressed because he or she is confronted with the idea of making changes in his or her life.

Because many children are unable to clearly and accurately express their emotional pain or feelings of deep sadness, some adults misinterpret these children's behavior as anger, acting out, or being unappreciative. Nevertheless, children are not exempted from experiencing depression. There have been reported cases of teenagers experiencing major depression, which led to roughly 10% of all American suicides. Major depression has also been interpreted as one of the motives for teenagers murdering their parents, and taking guns into schools, without an obvious reason.

Many people loosely use the term "depressed" when they feel sad, low-spirited, or as a reaction to negative activities occurring in their lives. Most of us, if not all, have said or heard someone close to us say, "I feel depressed."

At some point, in our lives, most of us will encounter some type of life crisis or tragedy. How we cope with our adversity, more often than not, reflects our mental health or mental illness.

As a social worker, I have interviewed and observed how people respond emotionally to various crises. I am reminded of numerous interviews during my private practice where clients were asked to think of a time in his or her life when they were most happy, or the moment that they experienced the most joy or excitement. Many were unable to think of a single experience, which made them feel happy. In many cases, these were individuals who had reported being abandoned by their biological parents, abused as children, and struggled with low self-esteem throughout their childhood and adult lives.

Much of my caseload with clients struggling with recurring episodes of depression often reported problems sleeping, difficulty coping with deep sadness, and feelings of emptiness during the holidays, especially around Thanksgiving and Christmas.

During the earlier part of my social work career, as an individual, marriage, and family counselor, I met many people who viewed seeking medical treatment for a physical ailment as less of a stigma. A few individuals were unwilling to accept a referral to a psychiatrist for early signs of depression or any form of mental illness. Of course, there were also those who would not seek medical assistance for physical, mental or any other health related issues. Unless, they suffered a broken bone or injury sustained in an accident, and had to be taken to a hospital. It is still quite surprising how many people, in the new millennium, are afraid to consult a doctor for medical attention.

A lot of research has been done, however, it is obvious that much more is required. Recently, an abundance of information has been reported about the increasing number of men, women and children being treated by medical doctors for depression, and the ratio of those receiving antidepressant medication.

According to information reported in the Journal of the American Medical Association, the number of people being treated for depression within the United States, jumped from 1.7 million to over six million, between 1987 and 1997.

The National Institute of Mental Health described depression as "one of the most common conditions associated with suicide in older adults, and is a widely under-recognized and untreated medical illness."

The National Institutes of Health published the following statement:

"Older Americans are disproportionately likely to die by suicide. Comprising only 13 percent of the U.S. population, individuals age 65 and older accounted for 18 percent of all suicide deaths in 2000. Among the highest rates (when categorized by gender and race) were white men age 85 and older: 59 deaths per 100,000 persons in 2000, more than five times the national U.S. rate of 10.6 per 100,000."

NIH Publication No. 03-4593
Printed January 2001
Revised May 2003

Most of the statistical data, published research studies, and findings based on the experience of mental health professionals all seems to agree that depression is a serious illness, which cuts across the socio-economic gamut without regards to race, color, gender, or economic status.

Beyond the use of lithium, during the sixties, seventies, and earlier part of the eighties, psychotherapy was considered a popular choice for treatment of depression. I believed that psychotherapy is effective in treating some forms of depression. By allowing the individual an opportunity to explore his/her feelings and the circumstances which might have contributed to their depression.

The studies reporting an increasing number of people seeking medical treatment for depression are encouraging. Many of the new research studies, however have also reported various unwanted side effects. Revealing that some antidepressant drugs inhibit sexual desires, or can cause prolonged sexual dysfunction in adults, and is believed to have caused suicidal behavior in children.

In addition to seeing a physician for a complete medical examination, everyone encountering depression and other mood disorders should also talk to a mental health professional and discuss the best treatment options for their particular situation.

A person experiencing depression for a long period, and one which is recurring, should seek immediate assistance. They should also seek some form of counseling or psychotherapy in addition to taking their medication.

The importance of diet and exercise should also be considered for mild depression and to reduce stress.

Recent studies have also reported the importance of rest and getting a solid eight hours of sleep.

Having a supportive family and a network of positive friends have also proven to be extremely important.

Regular aerobic exercise, walking, relaxation, and a planned nutritional diet have also been widely recommended for milder cases of depression. When in doubt, do not hesitate to seek professional help.

For more Information, please contact:

Postpartum Support International
927 North Kellogg Ave.
Santa Barbara, CA 93111
(805) 967-7636

Depression Awareness, Recognition, and Treatment
Program
National Institute of Mental Health
5600 Fishers Lane, Room 15C-05
Rockville, MD 20857
(800) 421-4211

The National Institute of Mental Health (NIMH) is reaching out to educate the public about depression in men through its Real Men Real Depression campaign.

For information about the NIMH Real Men. Real Depression. campaign:
Call toll-free: 1-866-227-6464
Or e-mail to: menanddepression@mail.nih.gov

Chapter IX

LIVING A REWARDING LIFE

During a discussion on "values and morality in America," someone asked, "If you had a choice between being rich even if it means living a complicated life, or live a modest, but calm, peaceful life with the love of family, friends, and community, which would you choose? Another person asked, "How is it possible to have peace of mind or live a calm life if you are poor?"

Success is often measured by different standards within our society. Some measure success by material possessions, job title, income or financial status, political influence, physical attributes, or by their ability to win at the expense of someone else losing.

During our lifelong search for a "Pursuit of happiness" should we strive for success based on any of the above criteria?

Several case analysis and scientific studies show that many people are motivated by expectations of positive rewards from others, such as love, acceptance, approval, and friendship. Some seek popularity and other forms of recognition from public attention for their participation in sports, as a leader in their community, or for their political party affiliations. Case studies have described how some people engaged in moral or immoral activities as a means to achieve their goals. Yet there are many who quietly seek only spiritual awareness and find comfort in their faith.

My experience with many different kinds of people have taught me that most people have a deep and abiding desire to live a calm, peaceful life of contentment whether they are viewed as successful or not. Most just wanted to feel happy, loved, and guilt free.

Throughout my childhood, I heard sermons about how to live a good Christian life and receive your rewards in heaven. Repeatedly, I heard that the only way to enter heaven was through the "Grace of God," and to earn "God's Grace," one must live a rewarding life here on earth which pleases God. Some of the elders in the community where I grew up, also used to say, "And God will take care of the rest."

For several years, researchers have been studying the relationship between spirituality, mental, and physical health.

In 1976, I gave a lecture at Ferguson Library in Stamford, Connecticut, entitled, "Winners/Losers: How to Write Your Own Lifescript." Influenced by many of the sermons from my childhood, information about the healing relationship between the human mind, body, and soul, in addition to a few therapeutic methods regarding behavioral modifications, I attempted to define a rewarding life from a mental health perspective—as living a life that renders personal satisfaction. "To live a rewarding life, one must maintain a sense of harmony and balance between mind, body and spirit—emotionally, physically, and psychologically."

Experience had taught me that success can be illusive and was often based on one's ability, which does not always assure happiness. Whereas, to live a rewarding life, one must develop self-esteem, self-knowledge, self-realization, and a concern for the welfare of others.

As you may well imagine, as a social worker, I have met many people who were quite unhappy with their lives. Many of whom had achieved monetary success and amassed a wealth of materialism. I have also known many who appeared to be living an enjoyable and rewarding life, some were poor financially, but rich spiritually with love and the support of family and loyal friends.

By nature, all human beings have the same physiological and psychological needs. Including the need for personal growth and fulfillment. Human beings also learn from experiences and are taught certain attitudes, which cause different behaviors, or ways of achieving their individual needs. Because no two people experience a situation in exactly the same way, individuals are more likely to have different ways of looking at life and situations. What may be considered a rewarding life for one may not be acceptable to another.

For many, living a rewarding life involves helping others or doing something for a common good—a goal which can also be accomplished in many different ways.

Of course, there are people who perceive life as one long painful journey. They usually have one complaint after another about what is wrong with life and all human beings. In many instances, these are the same individuals who would refuse an opportunity to participate in efforts to ameliorate many of life's negative circumstances. Many, are so preoccupied with the negative aspects of life, that they are unable to see or accept the positive conditions occurring around them or within their own lives.

Some maintain the belief that life is about self-preservation, or "getting all that you can, for yourself," without any concerns about the welfare of others.

Some people prefer to cling to their negative or stereotypical way of thinking about others. Many of these individuals remain silent about the social ills of society, or use a part of their short life-span working assiduously to deny others their natural human rights.

There are also those who have encountered social, economic, racial, religious, and gender disparities since birth. Some of these individuals adopt the belief that they are unable to improve the conditions of their lives. Consequently, far too many, give up on their hopes, dreams, or aspirations for achieving a rewarding life.

I have heard so many people complain about feeling "cheated" in life, because they believed that they were "too poor, too fat, too skinny, too tall, too short, too black, too pale, too bald, too dumb or uneducated, or simply "not good at doing anything."

Many have encountered situations, which seems to suggest that the value of one's life is vastly predicated on one's outward appearance, rather than on the strength of one's character. Some believe that individuals viewed as physically attractive or sexually appealing are more likely to succeed in achieving a rewarding life, than individuals viewed as less physically appealing.

Many have said that they are not allowed to forget that human beings live in a society with consistent messages about beauty and materialism. One widely held belief, is that the more luxury items a person own, the more likely he/she will be recognized as living a successful and rewarding life. As a result, many feel trapped in a constant state of unhappiness while trying to live beyond their financial means.

In addition to acquiring material possessions, there are those who spend an enormous amount of time trying to imitate or emulate others. Some, even pays a great deal of money for plastic surgery to improve their physical appearance in an effort to feel accepted, and as their way of achieving a rewarding life.

Of course, we all know that judging a person solely on outward appearances can be deceptive. Especially, if the person has an ugly disposition or a hostile and negative attitude. Compared to an individual whom others may not view as physically attractive, but has a positive attitude and a gregarious personality.

How often have we heard someone say that in order to live a rewarding life, everyone should be employed with a "good job," married by the age of thirty, become parents, own a house, car, computer with internet services, and a color television with cable or digital service. Now, one might also ask, "How rewarding is life without a stable and secure financial statement or diversified portfolio held in perpetuity, in addition to an expense account, computer, wireless telephone, and designer clothing?"

With so many unanswered questions and conflicting messages about how to make life more rewardingly, it is not surprising that so many people are confused about their identity and role in life. Perhaps this is part of the answer to why so many are asking, "What is life all about?"

Everyone should realize that even though all human beings have the same basic needs, everybody is different and do not share the same values or morals. Even identical twins have differences. There are short people, tall people, thin, and obese. There are people from different cultures, religions, and racial backgrounds. Some people are born into poverty, some are born into wealth. Some grow up speaking english, many grow up speaking other languages. Some people like to be surrounded by a crowd of people, and some prefer solitude.

Within any society, there are cultural standards of acceptance, which some interprets as perfection. Like success, *perfection* can also be measured by different criteria. To the extent that few, if any, ever achieve the total sum of societal, cultural, or religious highest standards of moral and ethical behavior, I am convinced that all human beings have idiosyncrasies or character flaws which sometimes rub another person the wrong way. But no one can claim a monopoly on perfection. All human beings have strengths, weaknesses, and limitations.

When we compare the billions of years that human beings have existed, the life-span of a human being is relatively short, even if one should live to be 100.

All living human beings, share one thing in common, the gift of   "life." Whatever similarities, differences, or problems we experience during life, are all part of living as imperfect human beings, within our short life-spans.

Recognizing that life is short and human beings are imperfect creatures, it would appear that for the brief amount of time we are allowed to live, everyone should strive to live a rewarding life and allow others the opportunity to do likewise.

If the life you are living makes you feel happy and brings personal satisfaction or great pleasure, then you are living a rewarding life.

Conversations with people who said they like the life they were living, often revealed that their lives were filled with peace of mind, joy, excitement with activities and relationships that made them feel happy to be alive and eager to look towards the next day. The description of their lives indicated:

1. They had developed the ability to get along with others.

2. They had developed the ability to cope with varied degrees of stress, or at least manage how they respond to different kinds of stress.

3. They had learned how to live within their financial means by designing their lifestyles around their budget.

4. They had realistic goals and expectations for what they believed was required to make them feel contented. Many of them said they were grateful for what they have and never worried about what they don't have.

5.   Some of them had designed their lives around their religious or spiritual beliefs. I heard many of them say, "My life is based on faith."

Based on numerous conversations and observations of people who appeared to be living rewarding lives, I have noticed two distinct characteristics they were able to achieve:

1. Accept the life they inherited and build on their deficiencies.

2. Develop a pattern of positive thinking.

1. Accept the life you inherited

Statistical evidence will prove that a very wealthy person has the resources to buy the best educational opportunities, health care, real estate, car, designer clothing, vacations, and so forth. Nevertheless, in regards to human behavior and relationships, it is still important to ask the question——If a child is born into a wealthy family will their status determine his or her adulthood fate? Will financial resources make his or her life less complicated and more rewardingly? Again, the answer depends on one's point of view and individual circumstances.

Of course, most people are aware of stories about an individual's triumph over poverty, child abuse, and parental neglect.

I have interviewed many families struggling with poverty. Many were overworked and stressed out due to long hours of hard unsympathetic back breaking employment. Their life stories often reflected various forms of stress, hardships, and daily pressure that could easily be labeled as mental illness. To provide for their children, some of these parents worked two jobs in their effort to protect them from the same harsh conditions they had grown accustomed. Many of the children from these families grew up learning a number of appropriate coping mechanisms. Some were able to use their experiences as survival skills, and achieve success. Some of them excelled in academics, drama, or sports, which helped them earn scholarships to attend college. Many of these children also developed socially acceptable characteristics and healthy relationships, which allowed them to live very fulfilling and rewarding lives.

There have also been numerous stories reported about individuals born into a family endowed with material wealth, and described as "a loving family." Yet when the child grew into adolescence or adulthood, his or her life was over shadowed by social and emotional conflicts. I have interviewed several clients from families described as "well to do," who had succumbed to failure and drug addiction. Many of whom had been overly protected by parents who tried to shield them from the problems of life changes. As a result of their inability to cope with conflict and life's varied realities, some had attempted suicide. The most effective therapy for some of these clients occurred in a warm, supportive, and non-threatening group setting where they were allowed to confront conflict and develop realistic coping skills that enabled them to start achieving realistic goals. Afterwards, many of these individuals were able to discover their full potentials.

With the advent of test tube babies, surrogate mothers, and genetic engineering, some individuals and couples are able to select certain characteristics of their child, including gender. The on-going scientific research using a chemical substance found in chromosomes known as deoxyribonucleic acid (DNA), are discovering endless possibilities. No one, however, rich or poor, privileged or disadvantaged, can predict with certitude the outcome of a child's personality and behavioral response to various emotions, nor provide a map of life with an opportunity to ward off disaster, hardships, sickness, and other human tragedies.

Everyone should learn to accept the life they have inherited and strive to build upon it with education, perseverance, hard work, and fair play. All of which will contribute towards developing a rewarding life and a better society.

There are many who could make a significant contribution towards improving the quality of life for themselves and for others, if they realized the importance of their participation.

How many times have you heard someone say, "If I was born rich, I could live a good life," or "You have to be tall, slim, and beautiful to get a job that pays well," or "If I didn't have a disability, I could have been..."

John H. Johnson was not born rich, but he expanded his natural talents and skills to become an entrepreneur. He started "Ebony" magazine and became wealthy by making a literary contribution to the world.

Spud Webb was five-feet-seven inches tall and weighed 133 pounds. Tyrone "Muggsy" Bogues was only five-feet-three inches tall. With consistent practice and improving their skills to play basketball better than the average player, both, Mr. Webb and Mr. Bogues, made it to the National Basketball Association (NBA). A sport where height is a definite advantage. Both have been acknowledged as great NBA players. Mr. Bogues has been recorded as the "smallest player in the NBA history and one of the NBA's all-time leaders in assist-to-turnovers ratio. Mr. Webb is still recognized by many as the all-time best dunkers after winning the 1986 NBA's Slam Dunk Contest.

Since the 1998-99 NBA season, we have witnessed the athleticism of another talented player, Earl Boykins, five-feet-five, 133 pounds, currently playing for the Denver Nuggets with a 2004-05 season average of 12.4 points per game (ppg). Again, proving that you do not have to be tall to accomplish dreams.

Mother Teresa and Sojourner Truth did not become famous for their feminine good looks, but for having gentle hearts, bravery, and compassion for others.

Can you imagine Stevie Wonder pinning away in isolation because he accepted his blindness as a disability, rather than share his talents as the most soulful entertainer of our generation as well as a great humanitarian.

What can be said about the lessons we have learned from the life and legacy of Ray Charles Robinson(1930-2004). An African American male, born into poverty, became blind by the age of seven, orphaned, and forced to cope with segregation's Jim Crow laws, social injustices, and the other evils of racism. Yet he triumph over poverty, blindness, and various forms of discrimination, and became an international inspiration to the human race.

Suppose Hans Christian Andersen had decided not to write children's books due to his disability, or because he was ridiculed by others.

By accepting the life you have inherited or the conditions of your birth, you learn to accept yourself for who you are and what you are—your limitations, as well as your capabilities.

There are so many ways to live a rewarding life, because everyone has something to offer.

If you are unable to become a world renown leader, become a community leader. If you cannot become a community leader, help others to lead. Even if you are poor, you have something to share. Your time, skills, and knowledge can be more valuable than money.

I am reminded of an elderly woman who lived to the ripe old age of 106. She was the daughter of sharecroppers. Her grandparents were slaves. Yet throughout her life she was known for her service to others as a church worker and community volunteer, and for her kindness towards her neighbors. Financially and materialistically she was poor throughout most of her life, but spiritually she was wealthy. When she reached the stage of her life where she could no longer do for others, there were many willing to do for her. From her point of view, she had lived a fulfilled and satisfied life.

2. Develop a pattern of positive thinking

Numerous stories have been told about how the quality of one's life was changed early in life due to poverty or the negative behavior of others. Some of the stories revealed how many were determined to not let their childhood trauma control their destinies. Many overcame their victimization by developing a pattern of positive thinking which enabled them to take control and live a rewarding life.

If you accept the premise that attitudes influence behavior, should it also be implied that one's thoughts can control his or her life.

In my 1976 speech, "Winners/Losers: How to Write Your Own Lifescript," I told the audience, it was always easier for us to blame others for our failures and hardships. The primary reason most of us fail, is due to our attitude, behavior, and the choices or decisions we make.

Scientific studies have revealed that negative thoughts stimulate negative attitudes and behavior, which often lead to delusional thoughts, irrational behavior, and poor judgement.

Positive thoughts, on the other hand, are more likely to lead to self-confidence, a calm demeanor, gregarious attitude, friendly disposition, and objectiveness.

It has been observed, within the study of phenomenology, that a negative thought can turn an untrue or unreal situation into one's own reality.

No matter what the scenario is, it would be wise to establish objective facts, by separating truth from fiction or fantasy based solely on fear or anxiety, suspicion or paranoia, prejudice, or hearsay evidence.

I think most people will agree that one's life would be much more enriched by living with positive thoughts, than those who hamper their personal growth by suffering needlessly with unsubstantiated negative thoughts and feelings.

Fear is an emotion or anxious feeling experienced in anticipation of a threat, danger, pain, or stressful event. Psychologists believes a bodily reaction to pain, stress, or fear, is a basic desire to either end it or avoid it, often referred to as the "fight or flight response."

When it comes to dealing with painful emotional or personal problems, some people chose to become pro-active by fighting or actively search for ways to resolve or end their problems. And some chose "flight" by running away from their problems, or simply blame others, or deny the fact that the problem exist and remain in denial.

Whether one chooses to cope with an emotional problem or run away, how you view your situation is very important. The ability to remain objective in a subjective situation is most often based on one's past experiences and on whether you view yourself or your situation from a positive or negative perspective.

Negative thoughts or pessimism can become a habit or a way of life, based on how and what you feel or think about yourself. If you think you are unworthy of a loving relationship, or will never find true happiness, it is quite likely, you never will.

Positive thoughts or optimism often reflects self-esteem—a positive sense of oneself, self-knowledge—an awareness or insight into oneself, and feelings of hope for the future. People who are living a rewarding life appears to be positive thinkers. If you believe that you are worthy of being loved and living a rewarding life, the chances are greater that you will.

As human beings, we have a choice to think negatively or positively, to live with defeat or to strive for a life of victories.

There are people who have lived the majority of their lives as victims. They often view themselves as helpless or powerless. They consistently choose to blame others for their misery and failure without realizing they are ultimately responsible for themselves.

If you were abandoned, neglected, abused, or betrayed, it would be in your best interest to move on with your life by refusing to allow what happened to you to control the remainder of your life. Dwelling on the negative aspects of your past often leads to viewing yourself as a victim. In most cases, reliving the negative memories of your past can often prolong the problem or produce other emotional, psychological, or physical problems, which prevents you from living a fulfilled and satisfied life.

No matter how difficult one's circumstances appear to be, one should always try to maintain a positive attitude with the belief that the rewards of life are well worth the short journey of our life-span.

Many of the clients who described their life from childhood to adulthood as negativistic—living with rejection, hostility, and various forms of abuse, quite often had their embittered behaviors reflected in their social, marital, and work relationships. Nonetheless, some of them expressed optimism about their future and were trying to make the most of their lives by either changing or adjusting to the external and internal causes of their behavior.

Just imagine the kind of world we would live in, if everyone took the time to think carefully, thoughtfully, and rationally before making a decision.

Decisions are based on an individual's ability to choose, and one should always remember that each choice has a consequence. I have often heard it said that "life is all about choices."

As a human being, you do have a choice as to how you would like to live your life, within the confines of the rules and regulations of your society. Unless you live under a dictatorial or some other form of an oppressive regime, it is your decision, to choose how you react to various situations or circumstances in your surroundings. It is your decision to choose how, if, and when others will be allowed to affect your feelings and attitudes. You must decide whether to change the circumstances which impacts your life or simply accept the circumstances as is and adjust your life accordingly. It is your choice. And it is your choice whether you define yourself as a winner or loser.

As part of the human growth and developmental stages of life, all human beings are granted the capacity to make decisions, and are expected to learn the difference between right and wrong, and accept the consequences of their actions. The exception to this rule would include individuals with congenital defects or other impairments which would hinder their decision-making abilities. Otherwise, once an individual grows into adulthood, they become responsible for their behavior, decisions, and quality of life, regardless of the external influences experienced during childhood.

It appears as though the demands of a rapidly growing technological society will continue to create stressful situations for many human beings, which will increasingly demand a positive outlook for personal growth and an ability to cope.

Technological advancement is inevitable, and is often recognized as human progress. Most people welcome the progress of medical and scientific research, although not everyone welcome the stress and anxiety from the pressure of everyday conflicts.

There are many who prefer to live a rewarding life based on the simple pleasures of life, which they believe can only be accomplished through their honesty, hard working accomplishments, good deeds, and the choices they make in life. Of course, there are numerous stories told by people who described how they achieved a rewarding life after they confronted a crisis, overcame a hardship, or survived the experience of a difficult struggle.

I have also known successful, strong, and confident individuals who were goal oriented and charismatic. They often described their lives from childhood to adulthood as filled with love, nurturing, encouragement, and acceptance. Yet they also had numerous questions about the meaning of life. Some of them described how they had to consistently make adjustments in order to maintain their emotional stability and a positive outlook on life.

Some positive thinkers view their problems as potential opportunities. Rather than feel discouraged or indulge in self-pity. I have listened to the details of how they also had to make plans to reduce stress in their lives, whether it was taking classes for self-improvement, exercising for physical fitness, or sharing quality time with family members, enthusiastic friends, and other positive thinking individuals. Many of them regularly made attempts to balance the negative activities occurring in their lives with positive influences.

Another thing I have consistently noticed—individuals who balanced the hardships occurring in their lives with a little fun, adventure, love, a positive outlook, and faith are often better able to maintain a sense of optimism.

During the earlier years of my social work training and experience, I had several questions about how human beings grow and develop; why we experience certain feelings; and what could I do as a social worker to help improve the lives of others.

My reading, research, and studies helped me learn various counseling methods of treating social, emotional, and learning problems. My social work practice and life experiences helped me gain the reality of how important it is for human beings to understand each other, and the many reasons why we should try harder to get along so that we can all live with peace and harmony.

My life experiences have also taught me that the most important aspect of human relationships is based on how we feel about ourselves, as well as how we relate to one another.

Hopefully, all human beings will live long enough to learn the answers to all of their questions about life, and mature into sufficient wisdom that will enable them to gain a greater understanding of the most rewarding aspects of life.

I strongly believe that if we learn how to love and appreciate the uniqueness of our individual lives, allow ourselves to search for the positive rather than the negative, we will help make life less complicated, and more rewarding for ourselves and all human beings.

The most rewarding gift any individual can offer during his or her life time is living a life that benefits all humanity.

Chapter 1. Notes On Life

Baltes, Paul. (1980). *Life-Span Developmental Psychology:* personality and socialization. New York: Academic Press.

Baltes, P.B., Reese, H.W., & Lipsitt, L.P. (1980). *Life-span Developmental Psychology.* Annual Review of Psychology. 31, 65-110.

Darwin, Charles (1859). *The Origin of Species.* London: Appleton.

Holy Bible. Authorized (King James)Version. (1970). Genesis, chapters 1 & 2. Philadelphia:The National Bible Press.

Johnson, James Weldon (1984). *The Creation.* New York: Holiday House, Inc.

Malthus, T.R. (1803).An Essay on the principle of population. London:Printed for J.Johnson, by T.Bensley.

Spencer, H. (1897). *The Principles of Sociology.* 2 Vols. New York: D.Appleton.
———(1969).[Original work published 1851] Social Statics. New York: A.M. Kelley.

Chapter II. Why People Behave As They Do ?

Ainsworth, M. D. (1982). *Attachment.* In C. M. Parkes & J. Stevenson-Hinde (Eds.), *The place of attachment in human behavior.* New York: Basic Books.

Berne, G. (1964). *Games People Play:* The psychology of human relationships. New York: Grove Press.

Buckley, K.W. (1989). Mechanical Man. John Broadus Watson and the Beginnings of Behaviorism. New York: The Guilford Press.

David, Jay (editor). *Growing Up Black*: The childhood experiences of
    nineteen African Americans. New York: Pocket Books,
    A division of Simon & Schuster, Inc.

Freud, S. (1935). *A general introduction to psychoanalysis.* New York:
    Washington Square Press.

Hall, C. & Lindzey, G. (1978). *Theories of Personality* (3rd ed.). New
    York: Wiley.

Locke, J. (1959). (Original work published c.1690). *An Essay
    Concerning Human Understanding.* New York: Dover
    Publication.

Maslow, A. H. (1967). *Self-actualization and Beyond.* In J.F.T.
    Bugenthal (ed.), Challenges of humanistic psychology. New
    York: McGraw-Hill.

Maslow, A.H. (1970). *Motivation and Personality* (2nd ed.). New
    York: Harper and Row.

Nye, R.D. (1981). *Three psychologies*: Perspective from Freud,
    Rogers, and Skinners (2nd ed.). Monterey, California:
    Brooks/Cole.

Pervin, L.A. (1984). *Personality* (4th ed.). New York: Wiley.

Piaget, J. (1932). *The Moral Judgment of the Child* . Trans. by
    Gabain, M. London: Kegan, Paul, Trench, Trubner, and Co.
    ———— . (1967). *Six Psychological Studies*. New York: Random
    House.

Skinner, B.F. (1971). Beyond freedom and dignity. New York: Alfred
    A. knopf, Inc.

Watson, J.B. (1914). *Behavior*: an introduction to comparative
    psychology. New York: H. Holt and Company

Chapter III. On Love and Sex

Dutton, D. G., & Aron, A. P. (1974). Some evidence for heightened sexual attraction under conditions of high anxiety. *Journal of Personality and Social Psychology*, 30: 510-517.

Freud, S. (1951). *Psychopathology of Everyday Life*. (A.A. Brill, Trans.). New York: Norton. (Original work published 1910).

Holy Bible. Authorized (King James) Version. (1970). *Christian Love,* 1 Corinthians 13. Philadelphia: The National Bible Press.
————*The song of Solomon,* chapters 1 & 2.

Katchadourian, H. A., & Lunde, D.T. (1972). *Fundamentals of human sexuality.* New York: Holt, Rinehart, and Winston, Inc.

Lewis, C.S. (1960). *The four Loves.* New York: Harcourt, Brace, Jovanovich.

Masters, W.H., & Johnson, V.E. (1966). *Human Sexual Response.* Boston: Little, Brown and Co.
————. (1970). *Human Sexual Inadequacy.* Boston: Little, Brown and Co.

Mims, F.H. & Swenson, M. (1980). *Sexuality: A nursing perspective.* New York: McGraw-Hill.

Reuben, D. (1971). *Everything you always wanted to know about sex—But were afraid to ask.* New York: Bantam Books, Inc.

Rubin, Z. (1973). *Liking and Loving: An invitation to social psychology.* New York: Holt, Rinehart and Winston.

Soble, A. (1998). *The Philosophy of Sex and Love: an introduction.* St. Paul, Minn.: Paragon House.

Vannoy, R. (1980). *Sex without love: a philosophical exploration.* Buffalo, New York: Prometheus.

Vatsyayana, M. (1963 ed.). *The Kama Sutra*. Trans. by Burton, R.F., and Arbuthnot, F.F. Medallion ed. New York: G. P. Putnam's Sons.

Chapter IV.   14 Notes on Marriage

Holtzworth-Munroe, A. & Jacobson, N.S. (1985). Casual attributions of married couples. *J. Pers. Soc. Psychol.* 48, 1398-1412.

Holy Bible. Authorized (King James) Version). (1970). Marriage and divorce, Matthew 19: 3-9, and Malachi 2:14-16.Philadelphia: The National Bible Press.

Lauer, J., & Lauer, R. (June 1985). Marriages Made to Last. *Psychol. Today*, pp. 22-26.

Chapter V.   10 "Old School" Notes on Parenting

Berne, E. (1961). *Transactional Analysis in Psychotherapy* A systematic individual and social psychiatry. Castle Books.

Comer, James, P., & Poussaint, A.F. (1976). *Black Child Care.* New York: Pocket Books.

Gordon, Thomas (1970). *P.E.T: Parent Effectiveness Training-* The tested new way to raise responsible children. New York: Peter H. Wyden, Inc.
———. (1976). *P.E.T. in Action.* "Inside P.E.T. Families: New problems, insights and solutions in Parent Effectiveness Training. New York: Wyden Books.

Grotevant, H.D., & Cooper, C.R. (1985). Patterns of interactions in family relationships and the development of identity explo ration in adolescence. *Child Develop.*, 56, 416-428.

Kunjufu, J. (1984). *Developing positive self-images and discipline in black children.* Chicago, Illinois: African American Images.

Lundsteen, S.W., & Tarrow, N.B. (1981). *Guiding Young Children's Learning* : a comprehensive approach to early childhood education. New York: McGraw-Hill Book Co.

Skinner, B.F. (1938). The *Behavior of Organisms:* An experimental analysis. New York: Appleton-Century-Crofts.

Zelnik, M. (1983). *Sexual Activity Among Adolescents.* In E.R. McAnarney (ed.). *Premature adolescent pregnancy and parenthood,* (pp. 21-36). New York: Grune & Stratton.

Chapter VI.   The Joy of Fatherhood

Cosby, Bill, & Poussaint, A.F. (1986). *Fatherhood.* New York: Doubleday.

Harrison, Harry (2000). *The Father to Son:* Life lessons on raising a boy. New York: Workman Publishing Co.

ILg, F.L., & Ames, L.B.(1955).*The Gesell Institute's Child Behavior:* From birth to ten. Chapter 12, Father-child relationship, (pp. 215-224). New York: Perennial Library, Harper & Row Publishers.

Popenoe, David (1996). *Life Without Father:* compelling new evidence that fatherhood and marriage are indispensable for the good of children and society.   New York: Martin Kessler Books.

Roker, Al (2001). *Don't Make Me Stop This Car.* New York: Simon & Schuster.

Sears, W. (1986). *Becoming A Father:* how to nurture and enjoy your family. Franklin Park, Ill: La Leche League International.

Chapter VII.   Notes on Family

Ball, E. (1998). *Slaves In The Family*. New York: Random House.

Billingsley, A. (1968). *Black Families In White America*. Englewood Cliffs, New Jersey: Prentice-Hall.

Boszormenyi-Nagy, I., & Framo, J.L. (1965). *Intensive Family Therapy*. New York: Harper & Row.

Farago, John & Sharon, (Leinwand, G. General editor). (1975). *The Family*. New York: Pocket Books.

Goldenberg, I., & Goldenberg, H. (1996). *Family Therapy:* "An overview." Pacific Grove: Brooks/Cole Publishing Co.

Haley, Alex (1976). *Roots*: The saga of an American family. New York: Doubleday.

Laing, R. D. (1971). *The politics of the family and other essays*. New York York: Vintage Books- A division of Random House, Inc.

Whitfield, C.L. (1987). *Healing The Child Within*: "Discovery and recovery for adult children of dysfunctional families." Pompano Beach, Florida: Health Communications, Inc.

Chapter VIII.   Coping with life crises

American Psychiatric Association (2000). *Post Traumatic Stress Disorder*. In the Diagnostic and Statistical Manual of Mental Disorders, 4th ed., text rev., pp. 463-472. Washington, DC: American Psychiatric Association.

Kubler-Ross, E. (1997). *The wheel of life*: "A memoir of living and dying." New York: Simon & Schuster.

Moon, Chris (1999). *One step beyond*. London: Mass Market Paperback.

Pelzer, D.J. (1999). *A Man named Dave*: "A story of triumph and for giveness." New York: Dutton.

Reeve, Christopher (2002). *Nothing is impossible*. "Reflections on a new life." New York: Random House, Inc.

Attention-Deficit Disorder

American Psychiatric Association (1980). Diagnostical and Statistical Manual of Mental Disorders (DSM-III-R, 3rd. ed.). Washington, DC: American Psychiatric Association.
———. (1994). Diagnostic and Statistical Manual of Mental Disorders, (4th ed.). Washington, DC: American Psychiatric Association.

Barkley, R. (1998). *Attention-Deficit Hyperactivity Disorders*: "A handbook for diagnosis and treatment." New York: Guilford Press.

Depression

Billings, A.G., & Moos, R.H. (1984). "Coping, stress, and social resources among adults with unipolar depression." *J. Pers. Soc. Psychol.*, 46, 877-891.
———. (1985). "Life stressors and social resources affect post-treatment outcomes among depressed patients." *J. Abnorm. Psychol.* 94, 140-153.

Sommers, M. (2000). *Everything You Need to Know About Bipolar Disorder and Manic Depressive Illness*. New York: Rosen Publishing Group.

Chapter IX.   Living A Rewarding Life

Carlson, R. (1997). *Don't Sweat the Small Stuff... and it's all small stuff*. "Simple ways to keep the little things from taking over your life." New York: Hyperion Press.

Covey, S.R. (1995). *First Things First*: "To live, to love, to learn, to leave a legacy." New York: Simon & Schuster.

Johnson, S. (1998). *Who Moved My Cheese?* : "An amazing way to deal with change in your work and in your life." New York: Putnam Publishing Group.

Kusher, H.S. (1982). *When Bad Things Happen To Good People*. Boston, Mass.: G.K. Hall.

Smiley, Tavis (2002). *Keeping The Faith*: "Stories of love, courage, healing and hope from Black America." New York: Doubleday & Co., Inc.

Vanzant, Iyanla (2001). *Living Through The Meantime* : "Learning to break the patterns of the past and begin the healing process. New York: Simon & Schuster Trade Paperback.

Acquired Immune Deficiency Syndrome: (AIDS) An infectious organism that is spread by bodily secretions, particularly blood and semen. The infection impedes the body's immune system, making it susceptible to developing various other infections.

Addiction: Devoting oneself and time habitually or compulsively in something.

Adjustment: An attempt to meet the external, environmental, or societal demands, and the internal demands of human nature.

Adolescence: The period or stage of human development preceding adulthood.

Adolescent: An individual who has reached puberty but is not yet an adult.

Adult: An individual who is fully developed and mature. A person who has reached legal age.

Adultery: Voluntary sexual relations between a married person and somebody other than his or her spouse.

Affection: A term used to describe warm, friendly, and caring feelings toward another.
Feelings of fondness or tenderness.

Afterlife: The continuing process of having life after the physiology of death.

Alzheimer's disease: a degenerative brain disorder of the central nervous system. One of the primary causes of dementia among the elderly.

Archaeology: The scientific study of ancient cultures, which includes a detailed study of buildings, graves, tools, and other artifacts from past human life and culture.

Attachment: A warm affectionate bond or reciprocal nurturing behavior established between two or more individuals. For example, the emotional bond between a parent and child.

Attention Deficit Hyperactivity Disorder (ADHD): A condition or syndrome characterized by one or all three types of behavior—hyperactivity, impulsivity, and distractibility.

Attitude: An opinion, personal view, or an expression of one's mood or condition learned or taught from experience.

Behavior: The way a person or group respond or react to a certain set of conditions or specified circumstances.

Behavior modification: A therapeutic approach that attempts to change somebody's behavior by rewarding desirable and acceptable responses.

Behavioral psychology: A branch of psychology based on the observation and modification of the way people behave.

Behavioral science: A field of science such as sociology, psychology, or anthropology that use scientific methods to study the behavior of humans and other living animals.

Bigamy: When a person marries another while still legally married to someone else.

Bipolar disorder: Fluctuates between two poles–manic (high energy) and depression (low energy). Characterized by recurring episodes of major depression and manic-depressive illness.

Birth: The passage of a human or animal from the mother's womb into the outside world.

Celibacy : A state of sexual abstinence for religious reasons or as a personal choice.

Cohabitation: A couple living together without being married to one another. Commonly referred to as "living together," or "shacking-up."

Commitment: A promise, agreement, or pledge made to a person, place, or thing.

Communication: A process of sharing and/or exchanging information, thoughts, ideas, feelings, and attitudes by one with another.

Conception: The fertilization of an egg by a sperm at the beginning of pregnancy.

Corporal punishment: Physical abuse. The striking of a person's body as a practice for discipline and punishment.

Counseling: A process of helping individuals deal with mild problems of social and emotional adjustment.

Crisis: A new situation or period in which things are very uncertain, difficult, or painful, requiring decision-making and behavioral adjustment.

Culture: A particular set of attitudes that characterizes a group of people whose shared customs, beliefs, and practices identify the particular place, class, or time to which they belong.

Defense Mechanisms: Based on a psychoanalytic theory that involves a method of mentally blocking harmful behavior to reduce one's internal anxiety.

Depression: An emotional state persisting for at least two weeks, characterized by feelings of hopelessness, dejection, poor concentration, lack of energy, and sleep irregularities. In extreme cases of a major depression, which may be recurring or prolonged, an individual may consider or attempt suicide.

Developmental psychology: A branch of psychology that studies the patterns of personality and behavioral changes during an individual's life span—between life and death.

Deoxyribonucleic Acid (DNA): Genetic information that determines the hereditary makeup of human cells.

Drive: A powerful need or instinct that motivates behavior. For example, the need to eat and drink are motivated by a hunger drive and a thirst drive. A heighten sense of arousal can stimulate a sex drive.

Dysfunctional: Failing to perform the function that is normally expected according to the rules and standards of a given group or society.

Emotion: A strong feeling about somebody or something that can affect behavior. Feelings that arise within a person such as shame, guilt, pity, anger, hate, love, or passion.

Epistemology: A philosophy theory concerned with the scientific study of the nature and origin of knowledge.

Family Therapy : A therapeutic technique used when all members of an immediate family is in treatment and the whole family is identified as the patient.

Feeling: An emotion or sensation perceived or experienced physically or mentally.

Frigid: To be cold or lacking warmth of feeling.
Inability to perform or enjoy sexual intercourse.
A term most often used to refer to women compared to "impotent" for males.

Genes: Microscopic particles composed of DNA, contained in chromosomes that are believed to be the basic elements for the transmission of hereditary characteristics.

Genetics: The scientific study of the transmission of genes and heredity.

Heredity: The passing on of genes and traits from parent to offspring, or from one generation to the next, resulting in similarities between members of a family.

Hoarding-to collect and store large quantities of unused or useless items, such as clothing, furniture, old magazines, and other possessions which clutters one's home or property.

Hormones: The secretion of chemical substances produced in the body's endocrine glands, which, when flowing through the blood-stream exerts a regulatory or stimulatory effect on bodily (physiological) activities.

Impotent: A term most often used to refer to men compared to **frigid.** To be cold or lacking in warmth, physical strength, or an inability to perform sexual intercourse.

Infancy: A term frequently used to denote the earliest stage, period, or year of human life.

Infant: A baby or child during its first year of life.

Infatuation: Spontaneous, but often short-lived passion or sexual attraction.

Instinct: An inborn (something acquired at birth) pattern of behavior that is unlearned, as opposed to behavior caused by experience.

Life: The interval between birth and death. The quality that makes living humans, animals, and plants different from dead organisms.

Love: A term loosely used to describe feelings of attraction, but often used to imply intense feelings of attraction, fondness and attachment for another person.

Marriage: The holy bond of matrimony. The recognized legal and holy union of a man and woman as husband and wife.

Mental illness: Psychiatric disorder of the mind, either congenital or induced by brain injury or disease that causes untypical behavior or impaired learning ability.

Monogamy: The practice or custom within a society of being married to only one person at a time.

Motive: The reason for doing something or behaving in a particular way. Often based on an impulse, emotion, physiological need, or desire.

Nature: The inherited genetic substance that is believed to help determine the behavior, character, and structure of an organism, as opposed to cultivation, or what is learned from experience and the environment.

Need: A condition or situation in which something is essential, necessary, or required. Such as food, water, air, and other basic human needs for growth and survival.

Neurology: A branch of medical science that deals with the structure and function of the nervous system, and the treatment of diseases and its disorders.

Neurotransmitter: Chemical substance that carry messages from the brain to different nerve cells or between nerve cells and muscles. These brain chemicals control human emotional responses—anger, fear, arousal, elation, and terror.

Nurture: Tender care and protection given to a young child, animal, or plant. Support and encouragement given to something to help it develop and grow.

Passion: A term used to describe an intense love for another person. It can also be used to refer to a strong liking or enthusiasm for something, sometimes of a sexual or excessive nature.

Pleasure center: The brain. The neurotransmitter or brain chemicals, when stimulated by touch, smell, taste, sight, or sound causes pleasant feelings, including sexual arousal.

Polygamy: The custom or practice of having more than one spouse at the same time.

Polygyny: The practice or custom of a man having more than one wife at the same time.

Post-Traumatic Stress Disorder (PTSD): A psychological condition that may affect people who have experienced severe emotional trauma, such as war, child abuse, sexual abuse, or the tragic death of a loved one.

Primogeniture: The eldest child (usually a son, in many class systems), granted the first-born status to inherit his parent's entire estate.

Psychotherapy: A technique used to help people with mental and emotional problems gain better insights into their personalities and relationships.

Puberty: The stage of human development when a person becomes physically capable of sexual reproduction, development of secondary sex characteristics, and, in girls, the first occurrence of menstruation. This stage also marks the beginning of adolescence.

Relationship: An emotional, psychological, verbal, and/or physical connection between two or more people. A condition of being related by blood, marriage, or similarity of behavior or feelings.

Space: An interval or period of time. The freedom or opportunity to assert a personal identity or fulfill personal needs separate from others.

Syndrome: a group of signs and symptoms that together form a recognizable pattern of a psychological disorder, or are characteristic of a specific disease.

Stress: Something that causes mental, emotional, or physical strain. The term often describes the anxiety, worry, and nervous apprehension related to a particular situation or event occurring in one's life.

Toddler: a young child between the ages of one and three.

Therapy: The treatment of physical, mental, or behavioral problems that is meant to cure or rehabilitate somebody.

Workaholic: A person who displays a compulsive need to work hard and for very long hours.